Phil H. Marquard
and
Cleveland's
"Homes Beautiful"

{Includes 2025 amended and updated content)

Thomas A. Marquard

ISBN-13: 978-1497546363
ISBN-10: 1497546362

First Trade Paperback Edition

2025 Edits, Updates & Index

Library of Congress Control Number: 2015909539
CreateSpace Independent Publishing Platform, North Charleston, SC

Biography/Non-Fiction

PRINTED IN THE U.S.A
BY
CREATESPACE AN AMAZON COMPANY

DEDICATION

This book is dedicated to the greats, grands, dads, moms,
uncles, aunts, sisters, brothers and cousins
especially
Doris Jeanne Faulhaber (1929–1995)
and my beloved brother
Timothy James Marquard (1950–1997)

CONTENTS

INTRODUCTION

It was around 1951 when I first remember seeing "The Big House." I was about four years old and huddled in the back seat of my dad's black 1950 Chevrolet DeLuxe, along with my older brother Phil and baby brother Tim. My father was Philip Frederick Marquard, the third eldest son and one of thirteen children of Philip Henry and Sophia Lindenau Marquard.

We drove slowly by the imposing mansion at 3260 Warren Road in Cleveland ogling the four stately corinthian fluted columns with elaborate capitals decorated with acanthus leaves and scrolls, guarding the front entrance. Dad told us that this used to be his family home. He had lived there for almost thirty years. With big eyes at the side window of the old Chevy, we were full of questions:

How many rooms does it have?
How old is the house?
Was your dad rich?
Is it haunted?
Are there secret panels?
What's the Depression?

Although it clearly was a mansion, I don't ever recall my father or any of his siblings using that term for the old house. They usually called it "The Big House" or the "Warren Road House." I think they were afraid they'd be viewed as snobbish or arrogant calling it a mansion. My Aunt Verona, Dad's eldest sister, constantly beseeched her siblings to stop calling it "The Big House," thinking that it too, sounded ostentatious. Or, maybe she was afraid the casual listener might think they had been in prison; often referred to as "the big house."

Over the years, with the addition of my sister Nancy and brother Gary, there would be five of us interrogating Dad for answers about our family history. He always got a little teary-eyed and choked up while trying to answer our shouted questions as we'd cruise by the mysterious old house. Usually he drove away quickly, after lamenting that the place was not being maintained and how he wished we could have seen it in the good old days; and how he missed his "Pa." He told us how the Marquard Building Company constructed thousands of homes all over Greater Cleveland. He would point out those houses as well as entire neighborhoods that they had built.

We lived in one of those homes in the suburb of Fairview Park and would frequently be in the vicinity of the old Big House while visiting relatives or stopping by "The Mill," as Dad and my many aunts and uncles usually referred to another family business, The Marquard Sash & Door Manufacturing Company. The Mill was also a place of fascination and questions for us little ones.

What the heck's a sash?
How come the mill doesn't have a big water wheel and apple cider?
Can we have some wood and nails to build a fort?

I came to learn that our history is not so much about the house and the businesses as it is about my grandfather, Philip Henry Marquard, his family and their lasting and significant contributions to society. From modest beginnings they applied their talents, skills and lots of hard work to achieve great things. The Big House is a bold reminder and a memorial to their dedication.

My grandfather passed away before I was born. To me he was heroic and somewhat of a mythical figure. I had heard many stories of his accomplishments, vast wealth, generosity and devotion to the Catholic Church. But above all, I knew from listening to the stories from my dad and his siblings, that their "Pa" was greatly loved and admired by them and many others.

Now, sixty-some years later, I believe I finally have answers to most of our questions and the many inquiries I've received over the years from curious Clevelanders. Surprisingly, there has been very little history written about the house or the family. So, I thought it would be a good idea to share the information I've collected while the revered old house is still standing, albeit on its last legs. (1)

I apologize in advance for the somewhat convoluted theme of this book. The project started out as a family history but very soon I knew it needed a more focused approach. I considered doing just a history of the Big House, but before long it dawned on me that the real story was my grandfather, his family and their "Homes Beautiful," which was one of their advertising mottos.

My cousin, the late Doris Faulhaber wrote two unpublished manuscripts. The first was a short biography of our uncle, David J. Marquard, the second was an autobiography titled "Tis Better To Have Lost." Unlike me, Dorie was a talented and accomplished writer who grew up in the Big House. Her writings were invaluable to me for this book. In many ways her influence inspired me to write family memoirs. I have included and attributed excerpts from her manuscripts throughout the book.

This is the story of a great man, his family and the big house in which they lived, against a historical backdrop of some of the best and worst times in America.

Thomas Austin Marquard
tamarquard@icloud.com

I. WHAT'S IN A NAME?

I think a good place to start this book is with our name which has always raised questions as to its origins. According to Archives.com, Marquard is rather uncommon, ranking 28,668th on the list of American surnames, with the largest concentration being found in Ohio. According to one source, in the year 2000 there were only 783 people with that last name living in the U.S. The Marquards are of German origin, having lived in and around Baden in southwestern Germany near the historically contested border of France's Alsace Lorraine region. The name itself means "Border Guard."

My father told me that, generally, we are related to all with the name spelled the same as ours as opposed to the many variations, the most common being Marquardt. The name has frequently been misspelled over the years by census takers, immigration officials and others. However, all evidence points to the correct and historic spelling as Marquard. Keep in mind that German family last names were not introduced until the late Middle Ages. There is some evidence that the name variations came about with the Protestant Reformation. Most with the "Marquard" spelling were Roman Catholic and have remained so.

My internet searches turned up some notable Marquards who may not be germane to this story, but nonetheless I've included here. My grandfather was a very devout Roman Catholic so there may be some clues to his faith since Catholic clergy Marquards abound. I don't know if these historic personages are related, but would like to think so.

Johannes Marquard of Munich evidently was a direct descendent of King Louis XIII of France.

Saint Marquard of Hildesheim

The earliest reference I found was Saint Marquard of Hildesheim. He was a Monk at New Corbey Abby, Saxony (modern Germany) and from 874 A.D. was Bishop of Hildesheim. Bishop Marquard was martyred in the winter of the year 880 in the battle at Luneberg Heath at Ebsdorf, Saxony. He was a member of the Army of King Louis III of France under the leadership of Duke Saint Bruno of Ebsdorf. He died along with three other bishops defending the local Christian population from the invading pagan Norsemen. The four bishops are known as the 'Martyrs of Ebsdorf'.

Marquard of Randeck 1296–1381

Born in Augsburg, son of a knight, appointed chancellor to emperor Charles IV at Avignon. In 1348 he was made prince-bishop of Augsburg. In 1355 he was sent to Pisa to suppress an anti-imperial revolt, during which he was wounded. Afterward he served as imperial captain and governor. Later Pope Urban VI gave him the title Patriarch of Aquileia. Marquard was able to quell all of the rebellions, recover all lost lands and force his enemies to make peace. After, he devoted himself to the war against the Republic of Venice until peace was achieved by the Treaty of Turin in 1381. He later became a prominent jurist and published the rules which regulated the law in Fruili, Italy. The code of law was known as Codex Marquardianus. He also restored the Basilica of Aquileia and rebuilt it in the Gothic style.

Marquard von Lindau

Marquard von Lindau is a little known figure. This obscurity is undeserved, not least because of his popularity in the fifteenth century. Around 450 manuscripts containing his works survive, which places him in the upper reaches of medieval bestsellers, a ranking very few can match. Marquard is of great interest for reasons other than his popularity. He was an innovative thinker, drawing on a wide range of traditions and sources but also pointing the way, in his use of them, to the sort of developments in practical theology later introduced by Martin Luther. Marquard, a Franciscan who died in 1392, is known to have been associated with the convent in Strasbourg in the early 1370s and later held the custody of Lake Constance, finally becoming provincial minister of the Franciscans in 1389.

Marquard Von Salzbach

(The following is excerpted from Wikipedia)

Marquard von Salzbach was a Teutonic Knight, who played a prominent role in shaping the relationship between the Knights and the Grand Duchy of Lithuania between 1389 and 1410.

He was taken captive in July 1384 by Vytautas, Grand Duke of Lithuania. At the time Marquard was a castellan of New Marienburg, a Teutonic Castle on the Neman River. Marquard became a friend and close adviser of Vytautas, who sent him on diplomatic missions to establish alliance with the Knights when another civil war broke out in Lithuania in 1389. Marquard regained freedom and rejoined the Knights, becoming castellan of Ragnit and valued expert of Lithuanian affairs due to his fluent command of the Lithuanian language and intimate knowledge of the royal court. When Vytautas turned against the Knights, Marquard fought against Lithuania in an attempt to conquer Samogitia. Marquard helped to negotiate the peace in the 1398 Treaty of Salynas and was able to bring 1,600 cavalry to support Vytautas in the 1399 Battle of the Vorskla River against the Golden Horde. The battle ended in a crushing defeat of the Lithuanians and Vytautas barely escaped alive. Of the Teutonic forces, only three knights escaped with a few low-ranking soldiers. Marquard accused Vytautas of treachery and almost derailed negotiations for the 1404 Peace of Raciąż. The personal conflict grew further, and was finally resolved during the 1410 Battle of Grunwald (Tannenburg), where Marquard participated as commander of Brandenburg. He was taken prisoner and then beheaded by Vytautas when he refused to apologize for the insult.

Baron Johann Marquard von Konigsegg 1450-?

Baron Johann married Princess Magdaleene zu and produced a long line of Barons and Countesses in the Baden region of Germany.

Prince-Bishop Marquard von Berg 1528-1591

Marquard von Berg was born in Opfingen, Germany in 1528. At the age of 13, he was sent to study at the University of Ingolstadt, where he remained until 1545. Starting in 1548, he studied law at the University of Padua and the University of Pavia. In 1551, he interrupted his studies to take over the parish church in Langweid am Lech. In 1559, he became provost of Bamberg Cathedral. He was elected Prince-Bishop of Augsburg in 1575 and Pope Gregory XIII confirmed his appointment.

Prince Bishop Marquard von Stauffenberg 1644-1693

Prince Bishop Marquard Sebastian Schenk von Stauffenberg was Bishop of Bamberg, Germany who in 1687 built the Seehof Palace, also known as Marquardsburg, as the summer residence of the prince-bishops. I have toured this palace and can attest to its grandeur. The Marquards seem to have home building in their blood.

It is also interesting that **Claus Philipp Maria Schenk Graf von Stauffenberg** was a direct descendent of Bishop Marquard. Colonel Claus von Stauffenberg (1907-1944), was a German army officer and aristocrat who was one of the leading members of the plot of 1944 to assassinate Adolf Hitler and remove the Nazi party from power. For his involvement in the operation he was shot shortly after the failed attempt known as Operation Valkyrie. Tom Cruise played his role in the 2008 movie "Valkyrie."

Bishop Marquard von Schenk von Castell 1605-1685
Bishop of Eichstat, Germany

Bishop Marquard Rudolf von Rodt 1644-1704
Bishop of Konstanz, Germany

Marquard Herrgott 1694-1762
Marquard entered the Benedictine Abbey of St. Blasien in the Black Forest of Germany and was ordained in 1718. He was a historian who wrote many scholarly religious manuscripts. In 1728 Marquard became a diplomatic representative to the Imperial Court of Vienna. He published a multi-volume complete history of the Austrian imperial family. In 1749 he offended the imperial family by defending the rights of the Church and lost his appointment. He later became Provost of Krozingen and Governor of Staufen and Kirchhofen, Germany.

Leo Marquard 1897-1974
Leo Marquard's father, the **Rev. J.J. Marquard,** founded **Marquard, South Africa** in 1905. Leo was awarded a Rhodes Scholarship to Oxford University where he graduated in 1923. In 1924 he founded The National

Union of South African Students (NUSAS) which was an important force for liberalism in South Africa in the latter part of the last century. Their mottos included non-racialism and non-sexism. From 1939-45 he helped in establishing the army education services and was promoted to the rank of lieutenant colonel and awarded the M.B.E. In 1945 he represented South Africa at the inaugural conference of UNESCO. From 1946—62 Leo was Editorial manager of The Oxford University Press, Cape Town, during which time he helped found the Liberal Party.

Richard 'Rube' Marquard 1886-1980

It may seem odd to include a baseball player in such august company as a Saint, knight and bishops; however in doing any internet research on the surname, no Marquard is more prevalent than the famous and colorful ballplayer. According to a 1914 news article my great Uncle Moritz Marquard was Rube's uncle so apparently I am related to the Hall of Famer.

The following is an excerpt from an article written by Larry Mansch...

"Tall and gangly, with a cannon for a left arm, Rube Marquard made headlines around the country in 1908 when the New York Giants purchased his contract for the unprecedented price of $11,000, by far the largest amount of money ever paid for a ballplayer. Marquard won a total of 73 games from 1911 to 1913, including a 19-game winning streak in 1912 that remains the record nearly a century later. He was referred to as the 'best left-handed pitcher in baseball.' With a wicked curveball to compliment his blazing fastball, and a fine screwball learned from his friend and roommate Christy Mathewson. Richard William Marquard was born in Cleveland."

Marquard Von Salzbach

Two versions of the Marquard coat of arms

Thomas A. Marquard

Seehof Palace

Summer residence of the Bamberg prince-bishops

"Marquardsburg"

1697-1803

Tour of the state rooms

The author at Marquardsburg in 2010

II. JOHN FREDERICK MARQUARD (1)
1801–1862

Stetten am Kalten Markt

Although there have been Marquards in the U.S. since the 18th century, my direct ancestors emigrated from Baden, Germany between 1848 and 1855. There's good evidence that the family came from the Stetten am Kalten Markt area, which is situated in Sigmaringen, Tubingen, Baden-Wurttemberg. At that time Germany was not yet unified and Baden was an independent state. Baden today is roughly the size of the state of Maryland. The town now known as Baden-Baden did not take that hyphenated name until 1932. Baden means "bath" as the area is a famous spa resort known since Roman times for its healing waters. Stetten am Kalten Markt means "place of the cold market." It lies about halfway between Zurich, Switzerland and Stuttgart, Germany. Today the population is around 5,000 and is home to a German security forces post.

Based on what I learned during my visit to the beautiful city of Baden-Baden, it is likely that the family may have fled Baden after the failed revolution of 1848, fearing harsh reprisals which included many executions. I was unable to locate any remaining Marquards in Baden-Baden. A local historian was familiar with the name but suggested that the entire clan may have fled after the 1848 revolution. Although I did travel extensively in Baden-Wurttemberg at the time of my visit in October of 2010, I did not know that the town I sought was, most likely, Stetten am Kalten Markt. Ancestry.com RootsWeb research reveals dozens of Marquard families in that town dating back to the early 17th century.

Baden's Rebellion

After 1806 Baden received a new government and in 1810, land reform after the French model. The constitution of 1818 and elected legislature were models for early German constitutionalism. The lower chamber was virtually a school for the Liberal-Nationalist movement. In April and September of 1848 there was rebellion under the leadership of the Left and in May of 1849 with the installation of a Republican regime, it came to revolution which Prussian troops had to put down. Severe punishment was meted out to the revolutionaries. In 1866 Baden turned back to constitutional ways.

John, Anna, Ursula & Children

I have learned quite a bit of the family's early history from Sarah Junke, a distant cousin, who's quite prolific on Ancestry.com and LDS's FamilySearch. She is the 3X great granddaughter of Anna Maria Marquard. Her sources revealed the Stetten am Kalten Markt family history. Those documents show that John married Anna Loffler (1801-1849)—my great-great-grandmother. According to the German documents they wed in 1828 in Stetten am Kalten Markt. Those records state that her father was Philipp Loffler (?-1824) and her mother, Magdalena Pfeiffer. Philipp's parents are shown as Jacob Loffler and Salome Kleiner, making them my 4X maternal great grandparents. (2)

John and Anna had nine children.

Anna Maria	1828-1890	m. John Vogatzer then Jacob Moehling
Bernhard	1832-1917	Framemaker m. Caroline
Conrad	1833-1895	Ice Co. m. Mary

Moritz	1837-1915	Cooper m. Magdalene & Katherine
Philip	1839-1907	Builder m. Mary Cerny
Jacob	1841-1913	Civil War Vet m. Mary
Charles/Karl	1843-1876	Civil War Vet
Joseph*	1844-1890	Civil War Vet m. Christine

* The first Joseph was born in 1836 and died the same year.

Tragically, Anna passed away, from yet unknown causes, at about age 36. John remarried in 1850 in Baden, to Ursula Haug (1815–1894). Ursula had a daughter, Mary/Maria Haug (1839–1907), apparently out of wedlock from a previous relationship.

Arrival in America

The best information I had on the arrival of the family in Cleveland came from research performed by my father's second cousin Wilfred B. Marquard and his son Robert, both of whom are now deceased.

Robert wrote me a letter back in 1996. Knowing that I was the historian in my family, he graciously summarized the results of his father's research which was gathered in the 1950s. He wrote that John was a widower when he arrived in the U.S., with seven sons and a daughter, between 1848 and 1854 and that the sea voyage took three months. New information tells us that John was already remarried when they emigrated. Wilfred named who he thought was the only daughter as Mary; however new sources indicate that there was a daughter and a stepdaughter. Anna Maria was John and Anna's eldest child and Mary was Ursula's daughter from an earlier relationship.

Much additional investigation has been conducted since Wilfred's, pre–internet, family history was written. My active search started back in the 1970s when my late brother Tim and I gathered information off of tombstones and searched records at old St. Mary's and Holy Cross Cemeteries in Cleveland. Much of this information is now readily available on the internet but it's no substitute for the memories of those days doing good old-fashioned detective work.

My great-great-grandfather, John, arrived in Cleveland from Baden, Germany between 1848 and 1855. So far, I have been unable to verify the immigration record or find definitive documentation on ship passenger lists. I have found likely records for the individual family members between 1850-1855, but not as a group traveling together. It may be that they did not all emigrate at the same time. The best evidence I have is the 1900 census which shows that sons Philip, Jacob and Moritz arrived in the U.S. from Baden in 1855. However, records show that their eldest sibling, Anna Maria, arrived in the United States through New York City in June 1853.

A note on a German emigration website warned that they only have records of legal departures from the country. Many that fled during or after the 1848 revolution may not have left by entirely legal means. Also, not all of the records from this era have been digitalized and must be requested in writing from the German authorities.

Ash Street

John purchased property known as sub lot 443 on Ash Street between Buckeye and Train Avenue in Brooklyn Township. The 1860 U.S. Census, which misspells the last name as Marqart, shows John's occupation as grocer, age 50, residing at 442 Ash Street with his wife Ursula age 45, along with sons Philip and Joseph. The same census lists his son Conrad, misspelled Marquart, living next door at

444 Ash with his wife Mary and son Philip J.

Wilfred's history states that John F. Marquard wed Mary Grotzinger; this is incorrect. It was John's stepdaughter Mary who wed John F. Grotzinger. Upon reviewing the 1860 Census, I found Mary Grotzinger, age 21, residing with her husband John Grotzinger and a two year old son William at 448 Ash Street, just down the road from John and Ursula Marquard. The Grotzingers were still married according to the 1870 U.S. Census but the 1900 census lists Mary Grotzinger as the widow of John Grotzinger.

Wilfred wrote that John's only daughter Mary wed a Vogatzer and then a Moehling. Once again, his sources appear to be mistaken. It was John and Anna's daughter Anna Maria—also known as "Mary"—that wed John Vogatzer (1824–1871) in Cleveland in July of 1853. The 1860 census shows them living across the street from John and Ursula at 439 Ash. Anna's husband is listed as a butcher. The only occupation I've found for John Marquard is grocer. Perhaps they worked together.

Cleveland city directories for 1882 and 1888 show Ursula as residing at 30 Ash Street and lists her as the widow of John. In both entries they misspell her last name as Marquart or Marquardt.

In 1905 Ash Street was renamed West 47th Street located between Clark and Train. That section of 47th Street still has many houses from the period. Cleveland's guide to the renaming and renumbering project does not show any three digit Ash Street addresses. It does show that 30 Ash became 3067 West 47th street but I was unable to determine if the house is still there. Adding to the confusion, I'm guessing there was an even earlier renumbering project and that 30 Ash may have previously been numbered 442, in which case it was the same house in which she resided with John in 1860.

Strained Relations

Wilfred writes in his history, "It is not known why his sons did not convey anything about their father to their children. It is believed that relations were strained when he remarried and apparently they were not on speaking terms." Ursula likely inherited all or most of John's estate after his death in 1862. According to Wilfred's notes, John's Last Will & Testament was drawn on June 4, 1861 and probated on March 2, 1862 as Case No. 547, Docket C. At least some of these records are now available on the internet but I was unable to locate the aforementioned. According to Sarah Junke's documents, when Ursula died in 1894 she left everything to her daughter Mary and nothing to John and Anna's children. This certainly could have added to or have been the cause of the apparent strained family relations. (3)

I have not been able to locate a tombstone or obituary for John or Ursula. Nor have I found any photos of them. See section at the end of the next chapter. Great-Great Grandfather John and his family belonged to the first Catholic Church in Cleveland, St. Mary's on the Flats. In 1854 the West Side Germans organized a parish of their own, naming it St. Mary's of the Assumption. For a while the parish used the older St. Mary's Church in the Flats. Under the pastorate of Rev. Fr. Stephen Falk the parish bought property at Jersey (now West 30th) and Carroll Streets and construction of a new church began in September, 1863. It was dedicated on Sept. 13, 1865. St. Mary's is where most of the early Marquards were baptized, married and buried. The church was demolished in 1968.

Germany 1855

III. PHILIP MARQUARD the First
1839–1907

I refer to my great grandfather as the First, making my grandfather the Second, my father the Third, my brother the Fourth and his son the Fifth. However my father told me that there were many previous Philips. I recall that he thought my brother was at least the Seventh. To further confuse an already very confusing family of Philips, my Uncle Marcus entered the priesthood and took the religious name of Fr. Philip Marquard.(4)

None of the records show a middle name for Great Grandfather Philip which was not unusual for the times although was unusual for the family. In what I believe is his 1839 Baptismal record from the Catholic Church in Stetten am Kalten Markt, his given name is spelled Philipp. Other early documents including his daughter Julia's wedding invitation contained the same German spelling. Some time later he adopted the conventional spelling of Philip.

Records indicate that Philip's father John was a grocer. Family lore has it that our forebears in Germany were known as fine craftsmen and cabinetmakers. This trait certainly was borne out by not only Philip but some of his brothers and certainly his offspring of which he had many.

Pioneer

Having arrived in Cleveland from Baden, Germany in 1855 at approximate age 15, Philip attended school and worked as a carpenter. The population of Cleveland at that time was around 17,000 and Cuyahoga County stood at 48,000.

Philip has been described as one of the oldest and best known pioneers and founders of Cleveland's West Side. He cleared the forest and with his own hands built their home around 1867 in what was then called Ohio City, later annexed by Cleveland. His home is still standing at what is now 4201 Bailey Avenue at the corner of West 42nd Street. Back then it was known as 28 Cook Street. Records reflect that at various times two of his brothers, Jacob and Moritz also lived on Cook.

Weds Mary Cerny

At about age 25, Philip wed Mary Cerny (1848–1920) on February 13, 1866 at St. Mary's of the Assumption. The wedding was officiated by Fr. Stephen Falk. Wilfred's history describes Mary as a "Slick Chick." I have no idea why he used that expression. Some old handwritten records appear to spell Mary's maiden name as "Carny" however the correct spelling was Cerny. The name Carny is likely Irish but Mary was born in Germany. Census records vary on her birthplace between Baden, Bohemia, Prussia and Hesse–Darmstadt. All of which are in the same region, with the exception of Bohemia.

Twelve Children

Philip and Mary brought twelve children into the world. Julia was born on May 3rd of 1866 or 1867. Most records say 1866 but some show 1867 and the 1900 Census lists 1868. I prefer to think it was 1867 as my grandfather, Philip Henry, was born in 1868.

Julia	1867–1931	m. Jos.H. Battes
Philip Henry	1868–1942	m.Sophia Lindenau
Frank Ben	1871–1893	Cause of death unknown
George Cooney	1873–1883	Cause of death unknown

John August	1874–1950	m.Gertrude Brickman
Ida Mary	1875–1957	m. Henry Lindenau
Joseph C.	1878–1947	m.Dorothy Spirnagle
Mary Katy (Mayme)	1880–1956	m. Dr. Louis J. Wise
Alma Lizzie	1881–1973	m. Wm. McAlleenan
William Jacob	1883–1883	lived only 7 months
Frederick J.	1884–1944	m. Laura Lindenau
Alphonse Joseph	1887–1890	Cause of death unknown

Carpenter and Builder

Philip was a carpenter and by 1869, a contractor and home builder thus beginning over a century of what became known as "Cleveland's Oldest Home Builders."

Wilfred's history recounts that in addition to houses he also worked on the construction of St. Stephen's Church. The following is excerpted from the St. Stephen's website:

"Recognizing the need for a second German nationality parish on Cleveland's West Side, Father Stephen Falk, pastor of St. Mary of the Assumption Parish secured property for the new parish. In 1869 St. Stephen Parish broke ground for a church-school on Courtlandt Street. In 1870 it celebrated its first Mass. Even though the parish celebrated Mass in the second floor church for the next six years, it soon realized that its growing membership required a larger church. In 1873, Bishop Gilmour blessed the cornerstone of the current St. Stephen Church. With many parishioners losing their jobs in the economic depression which gripped the United States in the mid-1870's, work on the project soon was halted. In order to complete the church, a number of parishioners put up houses, shops, and farms as collateral for a loan. Work on the structure soon proceeded, allowing the community to celebrate its first Mass in the unfinished church in 1876. Volunteering their services, German and Hungarian furniture-makers completed the church's wood interior, which contains hand-carved statues and stained-glass windows imported from Germany." The beautiful church is located at 1930 West 54th and is a National Historic Landmark.

Philip also worked on Holy Trinity Church in Avon, Ohio. Other projects included the Alpha Pharmacy Building at West 28th and Lorain as well as the old Jacob Mall/Gund Brewery.

Besides being President of the Philip Marquard Building Company, he was closely connected with a number of local societies and was a prominent member of the West Side Pioneers Association and the Builders Association.

In 1907, at age 68 Philip died from complications of the grippe—now known as influenza—in the home he built on Bailey Avenue. Mary continued living in the house until about 1914 when she and her son Joseph moved to a home built for them on her eldest son Phil's estate.

The Marquard-Battes Connection

In 1889 Philip and Mary's oldest child Julia H. married Joseph B. Battes (1866-1930). Joe was born in Germany and they had four children, Joe Jr., Jacob H. (1891-1947), Cecelia and Cornelius. The family resided on Carroll Avenue. Joe Sr. was a teamster/contractor according to the 1910 census. The 1920 census shows him as a foreman for the city street department. Joe Jr., who died in 1921, had been a bookkeeper for the Sash & Door.

Son Jacob H. Battes was the bookkeeper/auditor for the Marquard Real Estate & Building Company and later the Controller for the Sash & Door. PH's nephew "Jake" was a much loved and trusted advisor. Jake was married with children Mary, Helen, Philip and Catherine. They rented on Marquard property at 3282 Warren. By 1930 Jake was a widower, and by 1940 he had remarried to Loretta M. Paskert. The Paskerts were also close Marquard family friends. I believe Loretta was a widow as the census shows a child Mary Jo age 19 in addition to a son with Jake, Robert age 4.

My younger brother Tim married Loretta Manuel and much to the family's chagrin was the revelation that Loretta's grandfather was Jacob Battes! However relief reigned when research revealed that he was Jacob L. Battes not Jacob H. Battes. J.L. was Joseph Senior's brother, therefore there was no direct blood relationship.

J.L. Battes married Bertha Platten (1866–1938) and had a child Loretta (yes another Loretta!) who married James A. Manuel, who was born in Greece in 1893. James was a quite well-known candy maker who owned Manuel's Candies, having stores at various West Park locations over the years.

James and Loretta had one son James A. Manuel Jr. James and wife Kathleen bore five children one of whom, Loretta, married my brother Tim.

Where are John & Ursula?

To date we have been unable to locate a gravesite for John or Ursula. A headstone at St. Mary's marks the grave of Philip, wife Mary, son Frank and "Grandpa 1819–1892." I have confirmed by the dates that "Grandpa" was in fact Mary's father, John Cerny.

When my late brother Tim and I searched St. Mary's files years ago we pulled an index card for a "Grandma Marquard" (1839–1903) shown as buried in section 3, lot 89 north Gr. 2. We could not find a marker and today the

Find–a–Grave website for St. Mary's does not list a Grandma Marquard. I thought this might be Ursula's final resting place, however the dates of birth and death do not match Ursula's records. St. Mary's was unable to provide any further information.

Philip & Mary's former home at 4201 Bailey Ave in Cleveland (2014)

Philip at the wheel (1905 Peerless?) next to him Sophia with baby Cleo. Back seat: L-R Sophia's mother ?, Verona, Mary. Standing: Phil H., Olivia & Cyril. Ca. 1907
Below: Julia's 1889 wedding invitation

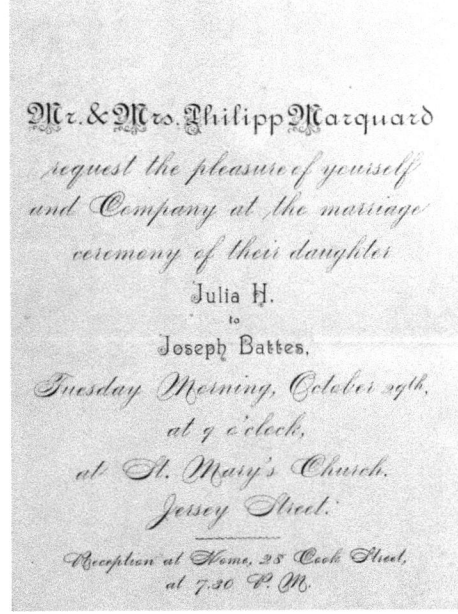

Mr. & Mrs. Philipp Marquard
request the pleasure of yourself
and Company at the marriage
ceremony of their daughter
Julia H.
to
Joseph Battes,
Tuesday Morning, October 29th,
at 9 o'clock,
at St. Mary's Church,
Jersey Street.

Reception at Home, 28 Cook Street,
at 7.30 P.M.

PLAIN DEALER
March 18, 1907

PIONEER IS DEAD.

Philip Marquard, one of the old residents of the West Side, who died Saturday night at his home at 4201 Bailey-av.

PLAIN DEALER
March 17, 1907

PIONEER IS GONE

Philip Marquard Helped Clear the West Side of Forest.

Philip Marquard, one of the pioneers and oldest residents of the West Side, died yesterday evening at his home, 4201 Bailey-av.

Mr. Marquard was one of the best known residents and a founder of the West Side, then known as Ohio City. He built his own home on the West Side when it was a forest and remodeled the house several times to keep in touch with the growth of the West Side. He died in the same place yesterday evening.

Mr. Marquard, who was sixty-eight years old, had been sick only a short time. An attack of the grip, on account of his age, caused other complications.

Mr. Marquard leaves a wife and eight children. He was president of the Philip Marquard Building Co. Philip H. Marquard of the Marquard Sash & Door Mfg. Co. is a son.

Decedent was closely connected with a number of local societies and was a prominent member of the West Side Pioneers' association and also a member of the builders' exchange.

Philip Marquard lays in state and the funeral procession from his home to St. Mary's Cemetery.

IV. PHILIP HENRY MARQUARD-THE EARLY YEARS

My grandfather was born August 18, 1868, the eldest male and second born of the twelve children of Philip and Mary. He always used the name "Phil H." to avoid confusion with his well-known father, Philip. On some documents he placed a period after Phil. Often he was simply referred to as PH or PHM.

I'm not sure how much schooling he received but it's likely he completed high school. According to Cleveland city directories, he worked as an agent, salesman, door maker or a machinist in those early years. I'm assuming that he learned his trade working with his father's building business.

My dad related to me that around 1885 his "Pa" went to work for the A. Teachout Company which was a lumber and supply business, as well as a sash and door factory. It was located in Cleveland at 301-317 Canal Road at West 3rd Street. Owing to his hard work and skill, before long he was promoted to foreman of the mill. Family lore says that Phil discovered a very successful formula and process to preserve and protect wood. He would not divulge the secret formula to Teachout. I worked at The Marquard Sash & Door the summer of 1965 and vividly recall the long metal trough filled with that mysterious preservative solution in which we immersed the raw wood.

Establishes Marquard Sash & Door

It was an era that spawned bold dreams and Grandfather dreamed of opening his own mill. He hammered out an arrangement with Teachout to purchase the unprofitable mill operation that occupied four floors of the six-story Teachout building. In 1890, at the age of 22 he realized his dream and established The Marquard Sash & Door Manufacturing Company, the genesis of his decades long business empire.

By 1890 Cleveland had emerged as the 10th largest city in America with a population that soared from 17,000 in 1850 to an astounding 261,000! The city needed all the product that Marquard could produce. The company motto was "If Its Wood We Make It!"

Phil H. suffered a major setback in September of 1900 when a fire, of an unknown cause, broke out in the early morning hours causing extensive damage to the building and contents. However, the building was still owned by Teachout and his loss was estimated at $15,000. Marquard's loss was primarily machinery and stock and was also estimated at $15,000, of which $7,000 was covered by insurance. This was the first of a number of fires that would strike the mill over the years. Being a builder Grandfather rebuilt and carried on.

Weds Sophia Lindenau

PH married Sophia Helen Lindenau August 24, 1899 officiated by Reverend Scheppach at St. Mary's on Jersey Street. The bride was age 23 and the groom 31. The marriage license misspelled Sophia's last name as "Linden." Sophia's father is shown as Henry and her mother as Amelia, maiden name Wellman. The bride's address is listed as 451 Columbus Street and Phil's as his father's home, 28 Cook (later known as 4201 Bailey). Sophia emigrated from Hesse, Germany in 1884 according to the 1910 U.S. Census.

The Marquard connection with the Lindenau family is interesting. Phil's younger brother Fred married Sophia's younger sister Laura. Phil's younger sister Ida married Sophia's brother Henry!

Cheaper by the Dozen?

According to the 1900 U.S. Census, the newlyweds were renting a house at 217 Taylor Street in Cleveland Township. There they started their brood of twelve children, the same as his parents. The family began on a sad note when little Evelyn succumbed in her first year from causes unknown. My father told me that there were actually thirteen children as he always counted another sibling who was stillborn and unnamed. I'm not sure in what year that occurred.

The following is a listing of their children.

Evelyn M.	1900-1900	Died in her 1st year
Cyrilus J.	1902-1922	Died of tuberculosis
Verona J.	1903-1990	m. Alfred C. DeCrane
Olivia G.	1905-2001	m. Edwin F. Faulhaber
Cleophas J.	1907-1976	Never married
Philip F.	1908-1968	m. Elizabeth G. Wertz
Adelbert M.	1910-1955	m. Bertha Wagner
Marcus J.	1912-1986	Fr. Philip O.F.M.
Vincent L.	1913-1986	m. Mary Jane Brennan
Francis J.	1915-1969	m. Sarah Jane McDowell
David J.	1916-1944	KIA WWII
Rita M.	1918-2003	m. Jack Sherer then Glenn Markle

The Jay Avenue Home

Grandfather only rented the home on Taylor Street (now West 45th) until about 1902 when he completed construction on the first of his "Homes Beautiful" for the family which was located at 2920 Jay Avenue, at the corner of West 30th Street in Ohio City (later annexed by Cleveland). Today the house is 3,600 square feet with five bedrooms and 4.5 baths. It had a ballroom on the third floor.

According to Aunt Honey's (Olivia) photo album, Cyril was born during the construction of this house. Verona, Olivia, Cleo, Philip and Adelbert were born in the Jay Avenue home. The 1910 census lists three servants, all of whom emigrated in 1889 from Germany. They were John and Katie Neuwirth, both age 44 and their daughter Katie, age 18.

After Grandfather's family moved from Jay to Warren Road, his brother John and family took ownership of the house and lived there for many years. I'm sure John had a lot to do with design and construction of the home.

Back in the early 1970s the Marquard house served as the American Indian Center. It was the first regional headquarters for the famous Indian activist, Russell Means, who was the director of the American Indian Movement (AIM). My brother Tim and I received a guided tour of the home during their tenure. In 1972 Means sued the Cleveland Indians baseball team for nine million dollars, alleging its Chief Wahoo mascot demeaned Native Americans. The case was settled out of court for $35,000. (4)

In recent years the house was purchased by Dave Stack who has had it meticulously restored to its former grandeur. The Ohio City Walking Tour map highlights it as the "Marquard Mansion." Some brochures refer to it as the "Marquard Castle" due to its turrets.

Early photos of Phil & Sophia (Marquard Collection) Below: Teachout Co. where PH established The Marquard Sash & Door in 1890 (CSU Memory Project)

ANOTHER again charming residence, this one with corner cupolas on second floor and dormer windows above.

1976

Home on Jay Ave. built by our Mother.
Verona, Honey, Elec Phil & Dorthy born here,
Mark, Vir, Fran, David & Rita born in big House
& girl born on 44th St. when house was being built on Jay

OHIO CITY, JAY AVENUE $194,900
MARQUARD MANSION
Second chance to acquire an Ohio City Landmark! 3600 sq. ft., w/
beautiful carved woodwork, inlaid floors, stained & leaded glass, grand
staircase. 3rd floor income suite + land! 820829
Jim Anderson   556-0330

CLEVELAND WEST HOMES • Sept. 12 - Sept. 18, 1996   61

The restored Marquard home at 2920 Jay Ave. (Courtesy of Dave Stack)

FIRE IN A PLANING MILL.

Flames Result in Damage to the Amount of $34,000 to a Canal Street Plant.

Fire broke out in the Marquard Sash & Door Co.'s plant at Nos. 172 and 174 Canal street shortly after 2 o'clock Monday morning and caused a loss of about $34,000 on the building and contents.

The cause of the fire is unknown. Two men are said to have been at work in the boiler room when the fire was discovered and one of the men is supposed to have turned in the alarm at 2:10 a. m. The fireboat was at its dock directly across the river behind the building and the boat company was about the first to get a stream on the fire. On account of the hill and the narrowness of Seneca and Canal streets the engines had considerable difficulty in getting to the fire. There were not enough fire plugs to furnish all the engines with water.

The fire burned for nearly an hour before the flames broke through the roof. At times the dense smoke thinned a little, and the fierce flames could be seen through the windows. It could be readily seen that the building would be gutted. Altogether about sixteen streams of water played on the fire through the widows, but seemed to have no effect in quenching the flames. The fire burned until 5 o'clock, but was under control at 4 a. m.

The building was owned by A. Teachout. It was worth $15,000. The building is not a total loss, and the loss is covered by insurance.

Phil H. Marquard, a West Side contractor, occupied four of the six stories of the building with a planing and finishing mill. His loss is $15,000, he says, and he had $7,000 insurance upon the stock. A large part of Marquard's loss is on machinery.

The loss entailed by the Cleveland Ornamental Glass Co., who occupied the upper floor, is about $4,000.

Left: 9/25/1900 PD Archives
Top: 8/22/1915 PD Archives

Application No. 20732   Filed and Marriage License issued   Aug 23" 1899

Name: Phil H. Marquard   Name: Sophia Linden
Age: 31   Residence: 28 Colok St   Age: 23   Residence: 451 Columbus St
Place of Birth: City   Place of Birth: Germany
Occupation: Merchant   Occupation: None
Father's Name: Philip Marquard   Father's Name: Henry Linden
Mother's Maiden Name: Mary Penney   Mother's Maiden Name: Amelia Kellman
Number of times previously married: None   Number of times previously married: None
Applicant: Phil H. Marquard   Married Name:
Marriage to be solemnized by: Rev. A. Scheppbach, Jersey St   License issued by: Frank Grislung
Consent of: Filed: 189   Consent of: Filed: 189

RETURN

The State of Ohio, Cuyahoga County, ss. I Certify, That on the 24 day of Aug 1899 Mr. Phil H. Marquard and Miss Sophia Linden were by me legally joined in marriage.
Rev. A. Scheppbach

Phil & Sophia's marriage record wherein her name is misspelled as "Linden"

The Marquard Company
Bungalow Specialists
Have Now Erected

23 cottages on all the lots of Newton-av. 17 of these buildings are now occupied by the purchasers. 6 beautiful bungalows are yet unsold. They are acknowledged to be THE BEST CONSTRUCTED SMALL HOUSES ever offered for sale in Cleveland. Artistic and modern in every detail. All street improvements (including nat. gas and electricity), are in and paid for. The fine location of this street—3 minutes north of Euclid-av and between E. 97th and 101st-sts—insures a select class of people. The property is also highly restricted. With down payments, deeds are given—the remainder may be paid in monthly installments not exceeding rent.

Don't miss this opportunity to secure a home right where you want to live. Open for inspection every afternoon. (

Princeton 1752 R.   C. A. MILLS, Sales Manager.

1911 Plain Dealer ad (PD Archives)

45

V. BUSINESS EXPANSION – A FAMILY AFFAIR

The Marquard Sash & Door Company was thriving by manufacturing and selling interior and exterior architectural millwork to institutions such as churches, schools, banks, libraries, public buildings and of course for homes in the ever-expanding Cleveland market. In addition to window sashes and doors the small mill on Canal Road was turning out everything from church altars to tavern bars. Many of the Cleveland area wooden church steeples were fashioned at the mill.

More profitable business emanated from wealthy Clevelanders who desired the fashionable stylish wood trim for their Gilded Age mansions. Customers clamored for Marquard's intricate custom craftwork. This market exploded not only in Ohio but as far away as Georgia and Florida. Phil brought on his brothers Fred and Joe to help him meet the demands of the bourgeoning business. Within a few years Fred became superintendent and Joe was general manager of the mill.

According to a 1902 Plain Dealer news article PH had emerged as a spokesman for Cleveland area mills and was instrumental in organizing an association to maintain prices and competition. He attended a national conference in Chicago establishing his reputation as an industry leader.

The Phil H. Marquard Real Estate & Building Co.

By 1906 Grandfather had expanded his business horizon and opened the Phil H. Marquard Real Estate & Building Company, continuing and expanding upon the firm founded by his father. The company would become known as "Cleveland's Oldest Home Builder," with its roots going back to 1869 and growing for over 100 years.

In 1907 PH's father Philip passed away so he enlisted

his younger brother John, who had worked alongside their father, to help run the business. John went on to become a master home builder. Phil was president and treasurer, John served as the company secretary, superintendent of construction and later as vice president. They opened the business at 1818 West 30th Street and advertised, "Will Draw Plans and Build to Suit You! Paying off same as Rent with only a Small Down Payment!"

The Phil H. Marquard Automobile & Supply Co.

Two businesses weren't enough to keep the young entrepreneur satisfied. Grandfather decided to try his hand at a totally unrelated line of work. The 1906 city directory lists him as the owner of The Phil H. Marquard Automobile & Supply Company. Automobiles were new and getting more popular and affordable for the masses and he, evidently, saw a future in the industry. The company advertising motto was, "Automobiles of Every Description Bought & Sold."

He was definitely a "Car Guy" judging by the many and varied fine automobiles he owned—as viewed in the old family photos. He had at least one car with PHM monogrammed on the door.

It was rare at the time for houses to have a garage. Not only did PH build homes with single garages, but his later home on Warren had an attached five-car garage in addition to a stand-alone two-car garage. Vin Marquard notated his family scrapbook that at one time the garages housed two Wintons, two Chandlers and one Ford. Later the deep garage would be for the family's Cadillac limousine. Apparently Grandfather believed in buying local, as the Chandlers (1913-1929) were built in Cleveland as were the Wintons (1896-1924). Grandpa may have been his own best customer.

Homes Beautiful

Based on the city directories it appears that Grandfather ran the automobile business until around 1919. Perhaps he decided to concentrate on his core businesses; the mill, real estate and building companies, which were all booming. That 1919 city directory—possibly for the first time—featured large advertisements for the Phil Marquard Real Estate & Building Company showcasing their new motto; "Homes Beautiful." A large 1924 advertisement was headed "Marquard Homes Beautiful." PH was a big believer in creative and eye-catching advertisements and was not afraid to spend the money necessary to get the public's attention.

VI. EARLY HISTORY OF THE BIG HOUSE

By 1908 the Phil H. Marquard Real Estate & Building Company was constructing homes all over the near West Side and the East Side of Cleveland. Following his father's pioneer spirit, PH saw the potential and future of the vast undeveloped property further west. He commenced buying up tracts of land to build the quality affordable bungalows for which the company was known at the time.

While on one of his land searches in 1907, he came across a picturesque farm for sale in what was then known as Rockport Village. In 1921 it became the City of West Park. It wasn't until 1922 that the 8,500 residents voted to merge with Cleveland.

Grandfather Buys a Farm

In January 1908, PH purchased the farm on 7.45 acres at 3260 Warren Road from the Brown family, for an unknown sum. In addition to the charming moderate-sized farmhouse there were two barns and other outbuildings.

Warren Road was originally an Indian trail. Henry Alger built the first cabin in 1812 not far from PH's land purchase. Alger was born in Warren, Connecticut that I thought might be where the name for the road originated. However I have since learned from West Park historian and author, Gary Swilik, that in 1858 the Marquard property was owned by Isaac Warren who is actually the namesake. Early family photos show that it was still a rutted narrow dirt road when Grandfather took ownership.

Jane Brown was the owner since at least 1874. The 1898 county atlas shows a cider mill on the edge of the property, presumably owned by the Browns. I'm not sure when the mill was removed. Deed records show that Mary C. Brown, Caroline P. Brown and Frances and Bradley

Bartter were involved in the sale. I'm guessing these ladies may have been Jane's daughters with Bradley being a son-in-law. The 1914 county atlas shows the property adjacent to the south of 3260 Warren as owned by Bartter.

According to my father the farmhouse was built in the late 1860s or early 70s. Grandfather used the original house as the nucleus of his mansion. This was confirmed by my cousin Vincent DeCrane, a retired architect, who grew up in the home. During a tour in 2010 he pointed out sections of the structure that were part of the original farmhouse.

Pleasant View

I'm not sure whether Grandfather's original intent was to make 3260 Warren his permanent family estate or if he just planned to enjoy it as a country retreat. It's also possible he desired the land to subdivide on which to build houses to sell. Later he did purchase property to the north, on both sides of Westland Avenue, which was plotted around 1912 for a subdivision, but not developed until many years later. Whatever the original reason, the Warren property evolved into his dream home and the Marquard family compound.

The precise date is unclear when the family made the permanent move from Jay Avenue to Warren Road, or "Pleasant View," as the eldest son Cyril once referred to the estate in his journal. In later years the family had a theatre/playhouse on the grounds and it was named "The Pleasant View Theatre." I don't know if the family came up with this name or if possibly it was the name of the original farm.

Historian and researcher Gary Swilik located a Cleveland Plain Dealer society news article dated June 23, 1912 which reads:

"Mrs. Phil H. Marquard entertained a party of her

friends at a garden party at Pleasant View, her summer home, at West Park, Thursday. The afternoon was spent playing cards, Luncheon was served in the dining room, which was embanked with white and pink peonies..."

So thanks to Gary Swilik we have evidence that the homestead was referred to as Pleasant View and was considered a summer home until the Marquards later made it their full-time residence. The name didn't stick as the family generally referred to the estate simply as "The Big House" or the "Warren Road house." However, I have located a photo from my Uncle Mark's album with a rare picture, from around 1927, of the theater and the name Pleasant View is clearly seen over the door.

The Family Settles In

We have photographs of the family at the Warren Road address dating from at least 1909, although the city directory does not list them as residing there until 1914. However, according to my Aunt Honey's (Olivia) notes Adelbert (Dauby) was the last child born on Jay Avenue in 1910 and that Marcus was the first child born in the Warren Road house in 1912. So the evidence points to 1912 as their residency date.

It appears they used the new place as a country or summer home while it was being remodeled and enlarged. The early photos of the fields, apple orchard, vineyards, barns, horses and chickens certainly look like farm life. From these photos it's hard to tell what the original home looked like as the house was transformed early on by Grandfather.

Interestingly, the estate once again became the Marquards' summer home in the early 1920s when the family built a winter home in Phoenix, Arizona. A 1923 Plain Dealer article described a charity benefit for the Villa Maria Academy held at the estate, that refers to it as

"Marquard's summer home."

Upon closer examination of the earliest photos of what I thought was the original house, I noticed a lot of Marquard trademark ornamentation. In particular, the 8-spoked sectioned railings along the front upper and lower porches. The design is the same as seen on porches shown on Marquard-built bungalows in 1910 real estate ads. Also, one of the homes built by Marquard on the estate has the identical unique railings. That same design was found in the window grillwork in the barn or coach house on the property as well as the children's playhouse. The transformation of the house was completed in many stages. The first stage looks entirely different from the finished product. I've been unable to find any good pictures of the house as it looked at the time of Grandfather's 1908 purchase.

County atlases show that PH had doubled his original purchase on Warren Road to include an additional lot on the south side measuring 163' X 680' as well as land stretching to the north side of Montrose Avenue, with that lot measuring 80 feet frontage and extending back 1,271 feet. His property on the west ended at 151st Street. Some of that property was slated for subdivision homes and The Regnatz Dining Hall. In a 1914 newspaper article the estate was described as "12 beautiful acres carefully laid out with lawns and gardens."

My cousin, Don Faulhaber, thought that at one time Grandfather owned up to 50 acres of land in and around the Warren Road estate. If true, I would think much of that land was for real estate development.

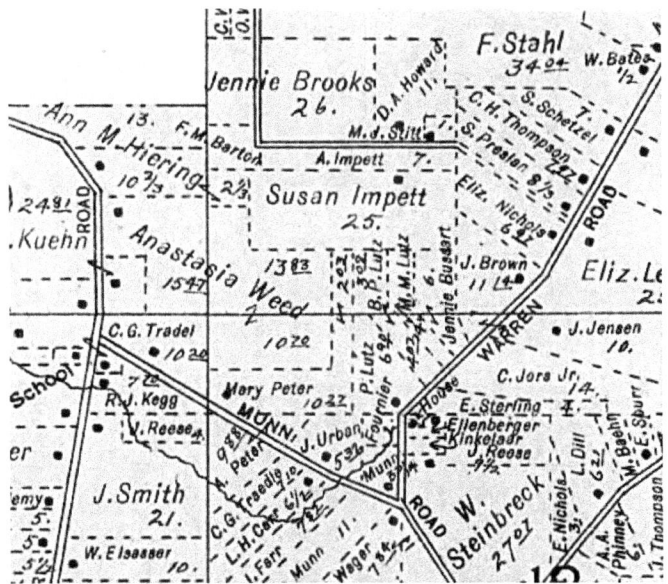

Top: 1903 Atlas shows J. Brown property at 3260 Warren.
Bottom: 1914 Atlas- center right shows P.H. purchase

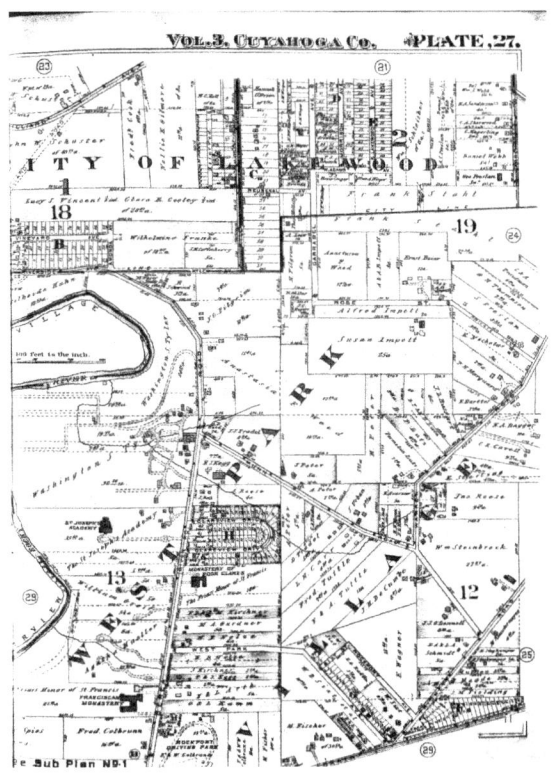

PH & Sophia at the gate of their Warren Rd. home ca. 1909

Above: L-R Verona, Olivia, Cleo (on hood), Philip & Cyril ca. 1910.
Below: Back seat Olivia, ?, ?,Verona, Cyril at the wheel, Adelbert.
Front: Philip & Cleo ca. 1911

Top: Warren Road in front of 3260 ca. 1909
Bottom: Notice the pedestal enhancements to the main gate.

Top: Family photo at Warren house ca. 1912
Bottom: Fred & Laura's house at 3276 Warren. Front: PH, Sophia. Second row:
Laura & Fred, Gertie & John , Grandma Mary smiling. Ca. 1912

Top: L-R Verona, Sophia, Olivia, Cyril, PH, Cleo, Philip, Adelbert, Laura &
Fred w/dtr Evelyn ca. 1911
Below: L-R: PH, Sophia, Cleo, Verona & Laura ca. 1912

Top: 3260 Warren Sophia on porch?
Below: Chicken coop on estate ca. 1910

Real estate ads ca. 1910
Right: Philip's brother Moritz a short
time before his death in 1915

HAVE YOU SEEN MISSING MAN?

MORITZ MARQUARD

Have you seen Moritz Marquard? At 77 years of age he is missing from his home, 3732 Bailey-av S. W. He left Monday afternoon at 1:30 for St. Mary's church, W. 30th-st and Carrol-av S. W., to attend mission service. He has not been seen since. His wife is on the verge of a breakdown. She is hysterical over his absence.

Mr. Marquard is an uncle of Rube Marquard, pitcher of the New York Giants and to Charles Marquard, councilman in the fourth ward.

PROMINENT REAL ESTATE MAN OF CLEVELAND

Phil H. Marquard, head of the Phil Marquard Real Estate and Building Company, 307 Canal road, is the pioneer bungalow builder of Cleveland. While never entering into the erection of cheap houses, Mr. Marquard has supplied the demand for bungalows of high grade, and several East End streets have been entirely built up by his company. Mr. Marquard believes that the bungalow is a staple type of house and is just as much in demand now as when it was more of a novelty.

The Phil Marquard Real Estate and Building Company is composed of Phil H., John A., Joseph C. and Fred J. Marquard. Each one of the brothers has charge of a particular branch of the business. The company operates its own factory under the name of the Marquard Sash and Door Manufacturing Company. It purchases the land in large tracts and erects the houses, producing the best grade of construction at a minimum cost.

The Phil Marquard Real Estate and Building Cmpany recently purchased the remaining lots on Bender avenue and will build it up with bungalows. The company has built up a section of E. 86th street, between Euclid and Hough avenues, and all of Newton avenue between E. 97th and

PHIL H MARQUARD

E. 101st streets. Mr. Marquard's company is a member of the Cleveland Real Estate Board and it has an enviable record in the city.

News clipping ca. 1911 (Marquard Family Collection)

MARQUARD FUNERAL TODAY.

Services at Church for West Sider Since 1855.

Funeral services for Jacob Marquard, 72, 4213 Bailey-av S. W., pioneer resident of Cleveland, who died Monday, will be held this morning at 10:30 o'clock from St. Mary's Catholic church.

Marquard was born in Baden, Germany, and came to Cleveland in 1855, settling on the West Side. He served in the civil war. He is survived by his widow, eight children and six grandchildren.

Above: Pleasant View Theater ca. 1914
Below: Theater ca. 1929 L-R: Fred, Cleo, Mrs. Regnatz?, Joe?, Phil F.

VII. BIG FAMILY IN A BIG HOUSE

By 1916 the family had grown to ten surviving children and life was good. Grandfather's business empire was growing along with Greater Cleveland, despite an earlier recession and a war raging in Europe. They were settled in their Warren Road home and were continually enlarging the estate.

Around 1911 PH's brother Fred and wife Laura had a large home built on the property at 3276 Warren, just south of the Big House. Although the home was owned by PH it was considered part of Fred's compensation for his work at the Sash & Door. Sometime after 1942 the house was expanded and today it is a ten-suite apartment house.

By 1914 a lovely home was built on the family compound for Phil's mother Mary, where she resided until her death in 1920. The house was in the rear, just west and south of the mansion and still stands today.* Her son Joseph and family lived with her until they moved to their own home on Granger Ave. in Lakewood—sometime around 1918. At various times afterward some of the married sons lived in that same house with their families.
*See Epilogue

The Chapel

The modest farmhouse was becoming a full-fledged mansion. By 1914 it had grown to at least 40 rooms. A chapel was added on the second floor replete with pews, altar and nearly life-size religious statuary. Bishop Joseph Schrembs of Cleveland consecrated the family chapel.

The following is the start of excerpts from my cousin Doris Faulhaber's (1929-1995) unpublished* manuscripts. She was Olivia and Ed's first born.

"Second to the ballroom in our affections was the chapel. It was a perfect little jewel of a room! The small, ornate altar was truly exquisite and richly fitted out for Mass. Grandpa invited his favorite Franciscan priests to read Mass for us on special occasions. The half dozen heavy oak church pews were smooth and highly varnished, and behind the door were dozens of nails with each of our rosaries hung there. After supper we would all troop up to the Chapel to recite the rosary together. You had to pay attention, because you never knew when you might be called upon to lead a decade or two.

On warm sunny days, the Chapel was the coolest spot around. We children would take off our shoes and socks and lie down flat on the satiny benches -- we would also scram away fast if we heard any adults approaching."... Dorie Faulhaber

My cousin and Godmother Clare Walsh (nee DeCrane), who also grew up in the house, told me how when supper was finished and it was getting dark outside, Grandfather would select one of the grandchildren to go upstairs and turn on the outside lights. She always cringed when it was her turn, as it was very scary going alone through the darkened upstairs halls and rooms to flip the light switch. She remembered how the wings on the chapel's angel statue would cast eerie shadows in the hallway of the big old house.

School and Recreation

The home had a schoolroom with desks for each of the children as well as blackboards. It was there that they did their homework, studied and practiced recitations. Maybe the old one-room schoolhouse around the corner on Alger Road was not large enough for all the Marquard children! The children did attend one or more of the local parish grade schools. The Catholic religion and quality education, along with hard work were family mainstays.

But it wasn't all beads and books for the children, quality play time was also important so PH constructed a grand park-like playground. In addition to the usual playground equipment there was a huge swing set that included elaborate animal-shaped gliders. The centerpiece was a giant wooden slide where two or three children could race each other while seated on burlap sacks. There was even a wooden roller coaster built for the thrill seekers! The estate also had its own tennis and handball courts. During our 2010 tour of the home, Vin DeCrane described a carpeted exercise room next to the third floor storage and baggage room that included various workout machines and equipment.

"We spent lots of time outdoors investigating the twelve acres or so that comprised our Grandfather's estate. We did reckless things on the adult size swings, see-saw, merry-go-round and chute-the-chutes."... Dorie Faulhaber

For a brief time there was an in-ground swimming pool but according to my father one of the little ones fell in and nearly drowned. "Pa" was so distraught over the accident that he called in a bulldozer and filled in the pool, converting it to a flower garden.

For indoor activity a two-lane bowling alley was housed in a separate structure on the grounds complete with pin-setting machines. Later the Pleasant View theatre and playhouse was added to stage plays and host charity social events. According to Vin DeCrane—the first-born grandchild—the theater was attached to the bowling alley, well behind the house and next to the tennis courts. It may be that the two-story barn or carriage house was transformed into the theater. Years later when the hardwood bowling alleys were dismantled, or perhaps replaced, one of the old alleys was used to construct or modify the playground slide. The other alley, according to cousin Vin, was used in a renovation to the interior second floor of the mansion.

Nature Lovers

Phil & Sophia had a real love for nature and that was reflected on the grounds of their estate. Besides the well kept lawns there were abundant rose and flower gardens tended to lovingly by Sophia, and Phil's mother, Mary. The home stood in a virtual forest of hardwood trees with flowering bushes and evergreens. Many of the trees and shrubs remain, although untended for many years. The giant sycamores and rhododendrons screened the house from the road after it was paved and widened.

This love of nature was passed along to the children. I recall how my father was able to name virtually every tree, flower and bush we'd come across. I especially remember being with my Uncle Mark sightseeing at President Andrew Jackson's Hermitage Plantation near Nashville, Tennessee, which had much exotic flora and how he would rattle off the names of the various species. Grandfather also loved birds and had quite a numerous array of elaborate birdhouses erected all around the property. They can be viewed in many of the photos of the grounds.

In August of 1914 a combination surprise 15th wedding anniversary for Phil and Sophia as well as 46th birthday party for Phil took place at the Rockport Club, with an after-party at the Warren Road estate. It was attended by many friends and relatives and received a glowing writeup in the Cleveland newspapers. Life was indeed good for the Marquard family. Contributing to their joy was the 1916 birth of another son, David. Within a few years their idyllic life would change considerably.

Fred & Laura Marquard's Home 3276 Warren Rd. built 1911
Bottom photo 1942

HONORED BY FRIENDS

MRS PHIL H MARQUARD

PHIL H. MARQUARD
Courtesy of Plain Dealer

cajoled by his wife into taking her to the club for dinner by way of celebrating the doubly important day.

Arrived there Mr. Marquard was confronted by the group of friends who wished him many happy returns and congratulated both him and Mrs. Marquard on their sixteenth wedding anniversary.

A savory and substantial chicken dinner was then served in the pavilion after which toasts were responded to by L. I. Litzler, Charles Gibson, Mrs. Mary Marquard, Mrs. E. Lindenau and William Marquard. Decorations were in lavender and white with vari-

FRIENDS SURPRISE PHIL H. MARQUARD ON HIS BIRTHDAY

Occasion also Commemorates Sixteenth Wedding Anniversary of Prominent West Side Couple.

BEAUTIFUL HOME IS THROWN OPEN

Dinner At Rockport Club Followed By Evening's Entertainment At Marquard Home—Estate Is One Of the Most Magnificent About Cleveland.

Mr. Phil H. Marquard, president of The Marquard Sash and Door Co., and the Phil Marquard Real Estate and Building Co., was honored by a large number of friends last Tuesday evening on the occasion of his forty-sixth birthday anniversary. The day also marked the sixteenth wedding anniversary of Mr. and Mrs. Marquard.

The party had foregathered at the Rockport club, and Mr. Marquard was

colored caps and table favors to match. In autos the party then went to the Marquard home on Warren road where they enjoyed the beautiful home and grounds, the bowling alleys especially proving attractive.

The Marquard home is one of the most magnificent in Cuyahoga county. It stands in the midst of 12 beautiful acres carefully laid out in lawns and gardens. It is of colonial design and contains some forty rooms. Mr. Marquard has eight children and it is his hobby to provide nice things for them. They have a school room, fully equipped with desks and blackboards, and on the third floor a chapel for their own use. In the winter they play in a sun porch, fifty by one hundred and fifty feet, all enclosed in glass.

Part of the grounds are devoted to a playground for the Marquard children. Swings, roller-coasters and all the devices of a modern play ground have been installed.

The bowling alleys, with pin setting machines, and complete in every detail, are in a separate building in the rear of the home.

Besides the Phil Marquard home, there is on his estate the houses of his brothers Fred and Joseph, and of his mother, Mrs. Mary Marquard.

Mr. and Mrs. Marquard received many beautiful gifts from their guests. Those for whom covers were laid at the dinner were: Mr. and Mrs. Phil H. Marquard, Mrs. Mary Marquard, Mrs. Elizabeth Lindenau, Mr. and Mrs. John Marquard, Mr. and Mrs. F. J. Marquard, Mr. and Mrs. Joseph Battes, Mr. and Mrs. P. J. Huegele, Mr. and Mrs. Henry Lindenau, Mr. and Mrs. L. I. Litzler, Mr. and Mrs. John Saxer, Mr. and Mrs. William Marquard, Mr. and Mrs. A. J. Reitz, Mr. and Mrs. E. A. Marquard, Miss Lyons, Mr. Emil Lindenau, Mr. Charles Gibson, Dr. E. Klaus.

Out of town guests were Dr. and Mrs. Louis J. Wise and Master Louis Wise of Akron, O.; Mrs. Lou Goldberg and son of Youngstown, O., and Miss 'enie Leindach of Baltimore.

Top: Sisters Laura & Sophia ca. 1909 (My favorite photo of Grandmother!)
Bottom: Note changes to house a few years later

Top: Verona, Cleo, Sophia, Olivia and Cyril with Philip on side. PH in background with Adelbert. The kids had their own coaster cars and giant slide ca. 1909.

Family photo on Warren Back: John, Gertie, PH, Sophia, Mother Mary.

Kids: Roland, Olivia, Philip, Verona, Cyril and Cleo ca. 1909.

Left: Cleo, Cyril, Sophia, Philip, Olivia. Mary & Verona ca. 1909

Middle: Joe & Mother Mary

Bottom: L-R Sophia, Marcus, Adelbert, Philip, Olivia, Cleo, Verona & Cyril ca. 1914

1914 news clipping (Marquard Family Collection)

The Chapel in the Marquard house ca. 1942

Top: Olivia ca. 1912

Middle: Sophia & Laura 1916

Bottom: Early photo of 3260 Warren ca. 1912

Top: 3260 Warren ca. 1911
Bot left: Trellis structure with birdhouses ca. 1915
Bot right: ca. 1915

Verona & Honey

Original playground equipment in orchard ca. 1910
Bottom left: PH, Sophia, Olivia, Cleo, Verona, Cyril ca. 1909

VIII. THE DARK DAYS

Loss of a Beloved Wife and Mother

Although the year dawned full of promise, it was not to last. On an unusually cold and snowy spring day, April 10, 1918, Phil and Sophia's last child, Rita Marie was born. She was a most welcome addition to a family of eight boys and now three girls. However the family's joy was cut short when Sophia became ill and passed away at age 41, on Friday May 31, 1918. My father told me her death resulted from complications from childbirth. The June 2, 1918 Cleveland Plain Dealer obituary states that she died at Charity Hospital and that "death resulted from an operation at the hospital." The funeral Mass took place at St. James in Lakewood at 9:30 AM on Tuesday June 4th. The death notice said that she was involved in several church and charity organizations. Grandmother is interred in the Marquard family crypt at St. Mary's Cemetery, which PH had erected for her with his own name in the prominent position. The cemetery is located at West 41st Street and Clark Avenue.

The sadness in the house was oppressive after the loss of their beloved "Mama", as the children always called her. She was Phil's wife for a short but wonderful 19 years. The oldest children Cyril 16, Verona 15 and Olivia 13, were called upon to help with the younger children and they took on many of the household duties. Their 71 year-old grandmother, Mary, was there to help but was somewhat hampered by her advanced age.

Fortunately Sophia's younger sister Laura, Fred's wife, lived just next door. In addition to her own five children (soon to be six), she stepped in and helped run the household. My dad always referred to his Aunt Laura with great affection, explaining how she had helped raise them after his mother's death. He was only nine years old when

when his mama died.

The family had a cook and two housekeepers, not a large staff considering the times and the size of their home and family. As earlier mentioned, at the much smaller Jay Avenue home they had three domestics. In 1920 the U.S. Census showed they kept the number to three live-in servants. They were Rosa Rung age 20, Ella Meister age 22 and Anna Threiner age 35. They were immigrants from Austria and Germany. The 1930 census listed three live-in maids: Marie Dagel, Julia Huddy, Marie Seraphin, and one cook: Augusta Polash.

Likely Francis & David at Mama's tomb 1918

ARRANGE MARQUARD BURIAL.

Services for Prominent Church Woman on Tuesday.

The funeral of Mrs. Phil H. Marquard, who died at Charity hospital Friday night, will be held at 9:30 a. m., Tuesday in St. James' church, 17514 Detroit avenue, Lakewood.

Death resulted from an operation at the hospital. Mr. Marquard is president of the Marquard Sash & Door & Real Estate Co. and is well known in West Park and Lakewood. Mrs. Marquard was interested in several church and charity organizations.

Top left: "Miss Hieman Took care of Mother and the babies"
Rt: Adelbert, PH, Cyril, Verona, Mary, Olivia, Philip, Cleo & Adelbert ca. 1910
Bottom: L-R Verona, Sophia,Olivia, Cyril, Cleo & Philip ca. 1916

PHM Hospitalized

I believe it wasn't long after Sophia's passing that Grandfather was hospitalized. The Cleveland Plain Dealer reported on his illness, however the articles did not reveal the cause other than to say his condition was serious. My Dad told me that at an early age Pa suffered a heart attack, so I'm guessing this was the illness written about by the newspaper. His condition caused him to seriously amend his lifestyle. He gave up smoking, swore off alcohol and followed a strict dietary regimen. He went so far as to commission a renowned German medical doctor to study him and prescribe a written detailed daily diet and instructions on how to live a long life.

I have the diet and lifestyle instructions. Oddly, the doctor's name does not appear on the manuscript. There are three typewritten sections, a total of 134 pages. The titles are as follows:

Section I. The Science of Brain & Bodybuilding Through a Vital and Rejuvenating Diet

Section II. & III. The Philosophy of Mental and Physical Fitness through Vital and Rejuvenating Foods and the Successful Relief of Complaints through Efficacious and Curative Dietaries of Dietetic Healing

Evidently, Grandfather strongly believed in these prescriptions and did his best to follow the advice. In his early photos he appeared to be a tall man built like a bull. In later photos he looks much slimmer and healthier. He lived into his 70s which wasn't bad for the times, especially for a man with a heart condition.

"I can still see Grandpa strolling, dressed in his pin-striped medium-brown suit with the gold chain across the high-buttoned vest, his huge diamond stick-pin in its customary place in the center of his tie. The thick reddish brown toupee he always wore (never saw him without it) defied the stiff breeze that helped him up the hill. Grandpa believed in "stretching his legs" in any kind of weather and it was fun to accompany him"...Dorie Faulhaber

Phil's Faith and Generosity

I believe Grandfather was always a religious and generous man but in the 1920s, 30s and 40s those virtues came to the forefront. I think it was a combination of having achieved wealth and having suffered great personal loss. Not only did this man have his own chapel but he did his utmost to attend the first daily Mass each morning, usually the sunrise service. He did this even when traveling. Son Cyril's journal of their trip out West in 1920 ,documents his daily Mass habit.

He was always known for his charitable acts, although much of the support he provided to a wide array of causes was anonymous. He was a principal supporter of local churches, notably Our Lady of Angels on Rocky River Drive in Cleveland. Another favorite was The Poor Clares Convent, and the Parmadale Children's Orphanage. Much of the work his companies performed for churches and other organizations was done on a gratis basis.

We have records of him donating huge marble statues in 1924, imported from Munich, Germany, to the new Our Lady of the Lake Catholic Seminary at 1227 Ansel Road in Cleveland. Later it became St. Mary's Seminary and in 1992, the Hitchcock Center for Women. Grandfather's charitable giving was not limited to cash donations nor restricted to the Cleveland area. He donated stained glass windows for St. Mary's College in Cincinnati and gave to charities as far away as Arizona and California.

In addition to being a 4th Degree Knight of Columbus, he accepted his proudest honor in 1928 when he received recognition from the Pope as a Knight Commander of Saint Gregory the Great. At an impressive ceremony in St. John's Cathedral, he was knighted by Bishop Schrembs with the sword being presented to him along with an octagonal gold cross which was hung around his neck. Monsignor McFadden read the Papal letter which was written in Latin on parchment. It read that the honor was bestowed in part because of his Christian life, his general charities, and among other things for his donation of the beautiful marble statues that adorn the entrance to the seminary on Ansel Road. It is the highest honor a layman can obtain from the Church. News items also reference him as being a Knight of St. John and belonging to the Moses Cleaveland General Assembly.

Grandfather Marquard was said to be an even-tempered man for the most part. Cousin Vin DeCrane related to me how the only time he recalls him raising his voice was on Sunday mornings when he was rousing all the children for Mass. It was tough getting the boys up and the girls often dawdled. PH always preferred the early morning services. He would roam the halls of the big house hollering for everyone to get moving or they'd be late. He finally solved the problem by installing a speaker system throughout the home. Vin said when he turned that volume up the kids would fly out of bed!

Grandfather's unshakable faith in God was soon to be tested in much more serious matters.

Cyril's Sickness

World War I was over and none of the Marquard brothers or sons had been of the age to serve, so the future should have been bright. However, sometime around 1919 the oldest child, 17 year-old Cyril, developed a persistent cough. His father had him examined by the finest doctors in Cleveland and he eventually was diagnosed as having tuberculosis or consumption as it was called back then. The sun's rays were thought to help the condition so Pa had a glassed-in solarium built on the rooftop of his mansion. Becoming more desperate to save his beloved son he prayed even harder than usual and sought out both medical and miraculous cures across the country.

On June 29, 1920 the family boarded a train and headed out West on a thinly-disguised vacation, seeking help for Cyril. They toured Chicago, Denver, Salt Lake City and Yellowstone National Park. Visits were made to Washington State, Oregon and the length of California down into Mexico.

Although they took in some of the finest attractions the West had to offer, they also spent many hours and days with various highly-recommended physicians as well as dozens of Catholic clergy. Many prayers were fervently recited at several different religious shrines. All in the hopes that Cyril might find relief from his illness.

While seeking medical and miraculous cures, PH's spare time was spent inspecting real estate in most every city they visited trying to find a climate amenable to his son's condition. It was not until they were headed home that he found what he sought. On July 27, 1920 the traveling party stopped off in Phoenix, Arizona. Cyril didn't know it at the time but the Valley of the Sun was destined to become their winter home for the next few years owing to the sunny arid climate.

The family returned home to Cleveland on August 2nd but it wasn't long after when PH bought land at 524 East McDowell Road in Phoenix and built another of his "Homes Beautiful."

For more on the epic Marquard family Western journey please refer to my 2013 book: "Trains, Plains & Automobiles."

In spite of his father's fervent prayers and best efforts to move heaven and earth, Cyril had only a few years remaining to him.

View of Sky Apartment 1943 Cleve. Press
Yosemite 1920 L-R: Cleo, PH, Olivia, Philip, Gertie, Verona & ?

Old Stage Coach   Hotel Mammoth

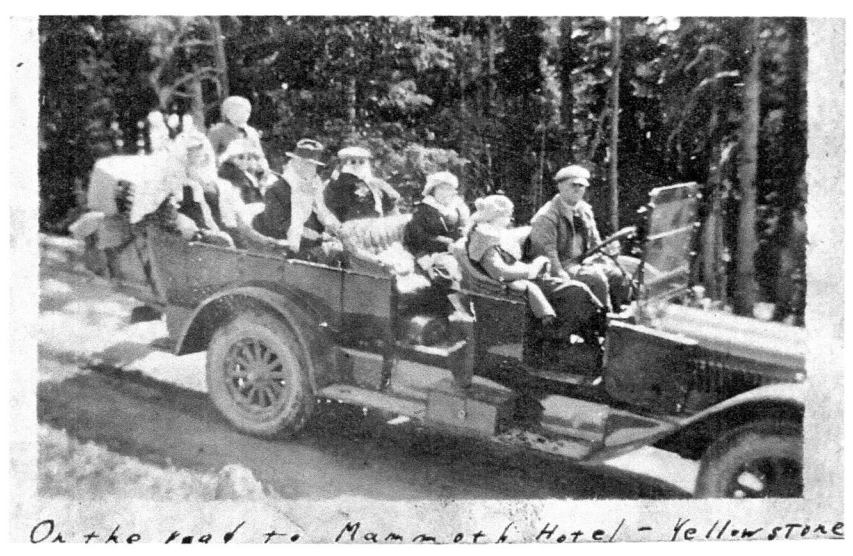

On the road to Mammoth Hotel - Yellowstone

The family out West 1920, bottom photos Cyril

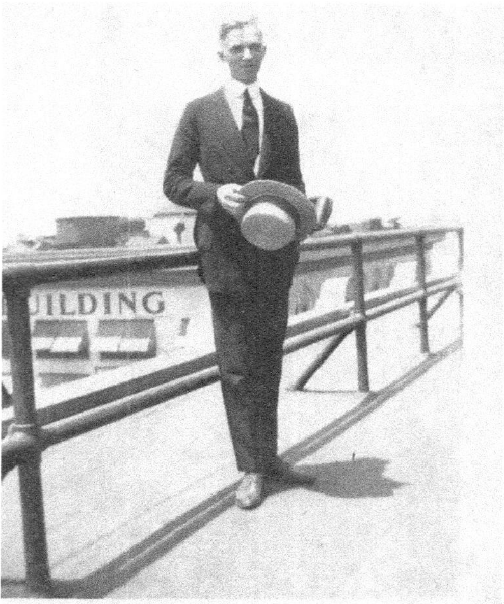
UILDING
otel Rosslyn roof Los Angeles

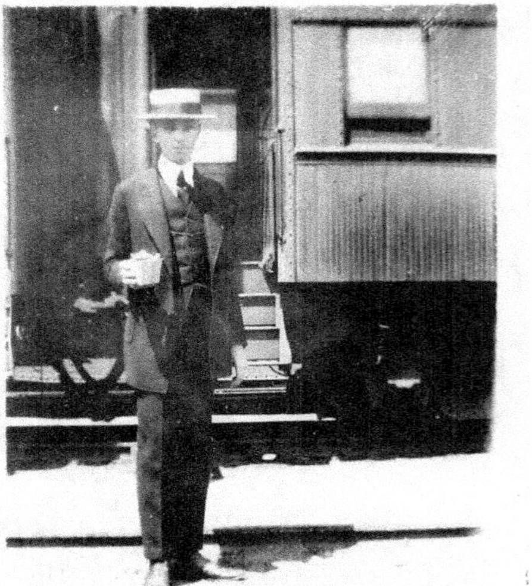
Cherries California

Mother Mary's Death

A month after the family returned from their trip West, Phil's mother Mary died at the age of 73. Great Grandmother Mary is seen in many of the old photos, usually at Sophia's side, working in the garden or with her grandchildren. It appears she took a very active role with the family. Having had twelve children herself, I imagine Sophia had relied quite a bit on her advice and assistance. After Sophia's death I'm sure Mary's role became even more important to the family. Once she was gone even more responsibility for the care of the children and household fell to the eldest daughter Verona, then age seventeen, and Olivia age fifteen. Thank goodness that the indispensable Aunt Laura was also nearby.

Mary, whose husband Philip (the first) died thirteen years earlier, was no stranger to family tragedy, four of her twelve children predeceased her. William at seven months, Al age three, George age ten and Frank age twenty-two. I'm unable to find any history on the cause of Mary's death or to that of her children referenced. Death often came early in those days from diseases for which inoculations had not yet been discovered; such as influenza, pneumonia and smallpox.

I remember my father telling me how, typically, when one of the children came down with something they all did. He also vividly recalled how one day the local doctor and a nurse arrived at the house and set up an operating room and performed preventive tonsillectomies on all of the children. Dad's words were, "He lined us up and yanked out our tonsils!" Afterward, they were all side-by-side in beds moaning and crying. What a sight that must have been and imagine the chore of caregiving during their recovery process.

Mary was buried at St. Mary's Cemetery next to her husband Philip, son Frank and "Grandpa" who was her father, John Cerny. I've been unable to locate the graves of the other children.

One can only imagine the toll all of this heartache was taking on Grandfather.

Sophia & Mary at 3260 Warren ca. 1912. Sophia, Mary (?) & Laura

Mary in front of home built for her on estate ca. 1914
Bottom: Recent photo of Mary's home

Grandmother Mary with Verona & Cyril in back ca. 1909

Below: 9/3/23 PD Archives

Mrs. Martin Sanders, dramatic read-
er, will be heard on Wednesday, after
a long absence, in a benefit program for
Villa Marie academy, Lowelville. The
entertainment will be given at the summer home of Mr. Phil Marquard, Warren road, Lakewood, under the auspices
of the Lourdes Guild.

IX. PHOENIX

In 1921 Grandfather Marquard bought three acres in Phoenix and built a large stately home at 524 East McDowell Road where the family spent most of the winter months. The hope was that the arid climate would improve Cyril's lung condition. Arizona had only received statehood less than ten years earlier and Phoenix, with a population of 29,000, still retained an aura of the Wild West. However the 1920s boom was happening there, just as it was in most of America's great cities. Over 1,000 new buildings went up that year in the city. St. Mary's was the only Catholic parish in Phoenix until 1928. Naturally, PH saw the vast potential and was keen on getting in on the residential and commercial development.

School Days

Although they lived within city limits, East McDowell Road was considered to be on the outskirts of town. My dad used to tell us stories of what Phoenix life was like in those days. We found one such tale quite amusing. It was how they had to walk through the desert to get to St. Mary's School. They wore high boots due to the prevalence of rattlesnakes. He and his brother Cleo, both in their early teens, convinced Pa to get them handguns to protect themselves and the girls from the poisonous snakes and other wild animals that roamed the area. Dad told us how he and the boys wore Buster Brown suits to school and how they were considered the well-regarded rich kids from "Back East." On one occasion when the teacher, I think her name was Sister Rosella, left the room, either Dad or Cleo fired off his pistol into the ceiling! He said they were never suspected of the wrong-doing due to their image as little angels in the nun's eyes.

It was while at St. Mary's, which was staffed by the Friars

of the Santa Barbara Parish, that son Marcus became interested in the Franciscan order and later would join those religious ranks.

The Winter Home

The family loved Phoenix and their beautiful winter home. The long ride out and back from Cleveland was made more comfortable via private railroad cars arranged for by PH. Many of the family and friends would join them on these trips, including the family doctor, Louis J. Wise M.D., who was married to Phil's sister Mary (Mayme). Dr. Wise also attended to Cyril's illness.

The grounds of the home were lushly landscaped with huge Royal Palms and other shade trees as well as flower beds and bougainvillea bushes. They had a 3-car garage, playground and stables for their horses. The children loved riding, a passion many of them continued into adulthood.

Grandfather deeply appreciated the Spanish architecture he found throughout the Southwest and California. He came to incorporate that style in many of the subsequent houses his company built in Greater Cleveland. One fine example is the home at 3256 Warren Road which was built in 1926 as a wedding present for his eldest daughter Verona and her husband Alfred C. DeCrane. It is situated next-door to 3260 Warren, on the north side. About this time the company also became well-known for building "California" bungalows and ranches. I'm not sure what involvement PH had in the design or building of the previously referenced Our Lady of the Lake Catholic Seminary in 1924; however, it too has a distinctive Southwestern Mission style. This was the church to which he donated the marble statues that adorn its entrance.

Although he loved the Southwest, the joy that was Phoenix was not to last much longer.

Standing L-R: Cyril, Verona, PH, Olivia, Mark & Cleo Sitting L-R; Adelbert, David, Philip, Rita, Vincent, & Francis ca. 1920

Views of the Marquard Phoenix home at 524 E. McDowell
Top is watercolor done by American Greeting Card artist Bruce Dicken

Top: Some of PH's & Fred & Laura's family gather at Phoenix home 1923

Marquard home 524 East McDowell Phoenix

Phoenix garage, with stables on left

Cyril's Passing

At approximately 11AM on Tuesday March 28, 1922 there was a total eclipse of the sun, which is described as "The total obscuring of the sun for viewers on Earth." It was on this same day and time that Cyril, at age 20, lost his battle with tuberculosis after an attack of influenza. He died at the Marquard home in Phoenix. Phil's first-born son was also obscured from viewers on Earth and the family once again went into mourning.

Cyril was a beloved son, brother and a very bright young man. He was a third year honor student in literature and law at Cleveland's St. Ignatius College. According to a news story, he was left "a small fortune by his mother and used the entire amount in works of charity, taking a particular interest in various charitable organizations he came in contact with throughout the country."

Ironically, when he first visited Phoenix during the 1920 family trip, he happened upon an Indian funeral procession at St. John's Mission and proceeded to join it as a mourner. Not even two years later, the St. John's Indian Mission Band led his own funeral procession. The wake was at the Phoenix home and after a brief interment he took his last train ride home to be buried in the family crypt alongside his mother and sister Evelyn.

The El Paso Texas Herald ran a news story that Cyril's father arranged to have a movie made of the various stages of the funeral so they could share the rituals with the family and friends back in Cleveland who were unable to attend. Apparently, this was one of the first times that a family funeral had been recorded in this fashion.

ARCH 29, 1922.

CYRIL J. MARQUARD DIES AT AGE OF 20

Cyril J. Marquard, aged 20, son of Phil Marquard, prominent lumber and mill man of Cleveland, Ohio, who recently took up his permanent residence in Phoenix, died at the Marquard home, 524 East McDowell road, at 11 o'clock yesterday morning. Tuberculosis contracted in the East more than a year ago after an attack of influenza, and aggravated by heart trouble which halted a recovery which had started, was the cause of his death. He passed away quietly while sleeping after a severe heart attack.

Young Marquard was a student at St. Ignatius college, conducted by the fathers of the Society of Jesus at Cleveland, before becoming ill, and had but one year of his collegiate course uncompleted at the time of his death. He had been an honor student during his entire stay at St. Ignatius, and his scholarship record, especially in literature and law, was unusually high.

He had been left a small fortune by his mother, who died about two years ago, and he used the entire amount in works of charity, taking particular interest in the various charitable institutions he came in contact with throughout the country.

Besides his father he leaves six brothers, Phillip, Adelbut, Marcus, Vincent, Francis and David; four sisters, Verona, Olivia, Cleo and Rita; an uncle and aunt, Mr. and Mrs. Fred J. Marquard, and a nephew and niece, Joseph and Evelyn.

Funeral arrangements have not been completed, it being undecided yesterday whether the body would be buried here or in Cleveland. Young Marquard was born on Feb. 26, 1902, in Cleveland, and was just 20 years and one month old at the time of his death.

―――o―――

BLIZZARD SWEEPS DAKOTA

FARGO, N. D., Mar. 28.—A blizzard, propelled by a 24-mile wind swept down across North Dakota and Northwestern Minnesota. The temperature at 7 p. m., was 11 below zero.

Funeral Services Filmed; Various Stages Are Taken

Phoenix, Ariz., April 7.—What is believed a new feature in film art was the taking of a moving picture of various stages of the funeral of Cyril J. Marquard, this by order of Phil H. Marquard, a Cleveland, Ohio, business man, who moved to Phoenix, hoping benefit to the health of his son, now deceased. Nearly 1000 feet of film was used in showing the services at the house, at the church and at the cemetery and the funeral procession, headed by the St. Johns Indian mission band. While the film was taken primarily as a family record, Mr. Marquard states also that he wished to send it east that it might give his friends a proper idea of Phoenix.

Sophia & Cyril ca. 1909

The Verona Apartments

Although PH remained very optimistic for Phoenix's future, the luster had faded now that Cyril was gone. We know the family continued to winter there for the next few years. But a short time later Grandfather had decided to turn the estate into a resort apartment complex. He converted the family two-story home and constructed seven new buildings into the thirteen-suite Verona Apartments, named for his eldest daughter. Additional landscaping and amenities made the property quite attractive and it enjoyed a fine reputation for quality housing. The resort complex became extremely popular with winter visitors and always had a long waiting list.

PH desired to further develop Phoenix; however, due to the extreme summer heat, still no main railroad line and more business than he could handle back in Cleveland, he decided to sell the apartments. In 1927 he sold the complex to J. Elmer Booth a newly-arrived investment developer from Rochester, New York, for the sum of $75,000. It appears, based on old documents that PH held the mortgage on the sale at least until the mid-1930s. I think he had thoughts of returning one day to pick up where he had left off. (5)

I first visited the Phoenix homesite around 1983. Although the structures were long gone many of the royal palms and bougainvillea were still in evidence. The once beautiful home and and grounds are now a strip mall.

Personals

, Marquard, with his ten
Irs. Fred Marquard and six
made a short stop at Albu-
meet Linus G. Wey, editor-
Mrs. Nick Arth and four
The Catholic Press Union,
way home to Cleveland
Mr. Marquard said the
east at Phoenix, Arizona,
party spent several months,
04 in the shade Monday.

rquard is having his Phoe-
changed into an apartment
ie will not again make use
is family during the school
lough he may still dupli-
his Cleveland and Lake-
evements of building fine
Phoenix should get a main
re. The Marquards are
ke for the southwest and
ir trip very much, but are
ever to come back to their
homes in West Park. Mr.
reports finding Mr. Wey
i health and a booster for
e where he found it.

Residence Style Apartment House

Here is a typical Phoenix apartment house built in the popular residence
favor with winter visitors as well as permanent residents. Note the beauti-
spacious driveway lined with graceful palms and the general home-life
sents the last word in apartment house construction.

WINTER VISITOR SHOWS FAITH IN PHOENIX FUTURE

J. Elmer Booth, Rochester, New York, set a record for 1927 in the buying of residential property in Phoenix yesterday when he purchased the Verona apartments, 524 East McDowell road, from Phil H. Marquard, Cleveland, Ohio. The unofficial price, as reported by persons familiar with the deal, was $75,000.

Mr. Booth has been in Phoenix for the past four months, and is enthusiastic over the prospects of this city as popular winter resort. He said that he purchased the property as an investment and that he plans to make a number of improvements on the place.

Mr. Marquard, who had owned the apartment for the past five years, had built them up from a single two-story building to a group of seven buildings, housing 13 apartments. The property has a 328-foot frontage on McDowell Road and is 300 feet deep. The arrangements of the buildings and the landscaping of the grounds make the property one of the beauty spots of Phoenix, and the group of apartment buildings is the most distinctive of its kind in Arizona.

"Phoenix has many advantages over the Florida cities," Booth declared after he had made the purchase. "and it will not be long before it becomes a great resort. The absence of humidity is a forceful drawing card, and the city in the summer is much more pleasant than the large eastern cities."

Booth expects to make the apartments ideal for summer, and to have them filled all the year around. Scores of applicants were turned away from the spacious apartments this winter.

The sale of the property was handled through Block and Burns, 15 East Adams street.

Verona Apartments Figure In $75,000 Deal

The Verona apartments at 524 East McDowell road which were purchased last week by J. Elmer Booth of Rochester, N. Y., for a consideration unofficially reported at $75,000. Mr. Booth is planning further beautification and landscaping of the grounds, already considered one of the beauty spots of the city.

Further Beautification Of Verona Ground Planned By Buyer Of Apartment House

Plans for further beautification of the Verona apartments at 524 East McDowell road are being made by J. Elmer Booth of Rochester, N. Y., who last week purchased the property in a sale which was unofficially reported to have involved a sum of $75,000. Mr. Booth has already completed arrangements with a landscaping architect for the carrying on of the work.

"The place already is one of the beauty spots of the city, but I believe other things can be done to add additional charm to the property. With its many shade trees, flowers and shrubbery already full grown, the task of further beautifying the grounds will not be a difficult one" Mr. Booth said.

Another plan of Mr. Booth is to establish the apartment house as an all-year-round institution. "In the past there has been a waiting list during the winter months and many vacancies in the summer. I believe with its large amount of shade trees and its location in a cool section of the city provides excellent advantages as an all-year-round apartment house and makes it an ideal place for summer residents of Phoenix. With this idea in mind we will make every effort to develop the Verona as an all-year place of residence."

The apartments were purchased from Phil H. Marquard of Cleveland, O., who has owned the property for more than five years. He has built it up from a single two-story building to a group of seven buildings containing 13 apartments. The property comprises approximately three acres having a frontage of 328 feet on McDowell road and a depth of 300 feet.

Mr. Booth, who has spent winters in Florida in the past, is a strong booster for the Salt River valley. "Phoenix has many advantages over the Florida cities and it will not be long before it becomes

A Dead Teacher

Sister Rosella on Thursday afternoon laid down the cross she had borne for many years to take up the well-earned crown. She had devoted a life to the highest calling it is given one in this world to follow. For thirteen years she had been a teacher in St. Mary's and during that time there had passed through her competent hands the plastic material which has been moulded into the younger members of the generation soon to be charged with the social and civic burdens of the community.

Forty-one years of her life had been given to this. The good she has wrought is incalculable. We can only partially measure it in those of her pupils whom

1927 Phoenix newspaper articles from family scrapbook

X. THE BOOMING TWENTIES

By 1920 Cleveland had nearly tripled in population since 1890 reaching 797,000. Cuyahoga County population was only slightly higher at 943,000 but that number was due to hit 1.2 million by 1930 as many were heading west. World War I was over and times were good. The rich were getting richer and the emerging middle class had some money and desired new homes. The Phil Marquard Real Estate & Building Company was there to meet their needs and The Marquard Sash & Door was working overtime to provide all of the architectural millwork.

New Market and Products

For years Marquard was known for building quality, modest and affordable homes. PH was the bungalow king. All that was changing as he shifted resources to Cleveland's West Side and to Lakewood. Apparently, Grandfather took Horace Greeley's advice when he wrote "Go West, young man, go West and grow up with the country!"

The Marquard brothers developed much of the lakefront property along Edgewater and Lake Avenues. The homes were larger, often custom-built and they had all of the modern conveniences. Vin DeCrane who is a graduate architect refers to Phil's brother John as a "Master Builder." Today that title, GMB or Graduate Master Builder requires a great deal of coursework and expertise. I don't know if John held the formal title and completed the coursework, assuming it was even available back in those days. But there is no doubt that he was a master builder and the chief architect with PH being the linchpin in the family enterprises.

I'm speculating that Phil had given his brother John free rein with these new homes and the results were extraordinary. In 1921 they teamed up with the Cleveland Electrical League to construct "Electric Servantless Homes." The second such home they built was located at 11320 Lake Avenue and garnered lots of press for its innovations. It was and remains one of many Marquard "Homes Beautiful." The 2,600 square foot four bedroom home sits on over a quarter acre of land. It boasted such innovations as a two-car garage with a concrete driveway. It had ninety-five electrical outlets including a switch in the master bedroom which could control all the lights in the house. There was an electric fireplace in the living room, a whole house built-in vacuum cleaner system, a lighted summer rooftop garden and even custom-built birdhouses!

Another beautiful Marquard home built about the same time stands at 11400 Lake Avenue. The Sash & Door architectural details are magnificent. Many of these new innovations were also installed at 3260 Warren, including the built-in vacuum cleaner system. By 1924 there were over 7,500 people living in Marquard homes.

In 1923 their ads started featuring the slogan "Never a Foreclosure." That policy would bring about huge problems in the next decade.

Announcing

The 2nd
Sept 11 to Oct 9
ELECTRICAL HOME

Open for Public Inspection

TODAY

And for One Month Each Day
From 1 P. M. to 10 P. M.

More than 34,000 people inspected the first Cleveland Electrical Home, opened for one month last May. So popular was this unusual "Servant-less" structure that the Electrical League has undertaken the display of another Electrical Home, even more completely furnished electrically than the first.

The home is the last word in the most modern electrical labor-saving equipment and scientific illumination. It was planned throughout by the best available experts in the country. A corps of demonstrators has been engaged to explain each separate feature to visitors.

The Electrical Home idea is a part of the Electrical League's year's educational campaign. The construction of the second home was accomplished through the co-operation of the Phil Marquard Real Estate & Building Co., the builders, and the Young Furniture Co., which installed the furniture and draperies.

Located at
11320 Lake Avenue
Take Clifton Car to W. 111th Street
Follow the Arrows

Electrical League of Cleveland

Plans of Newest Electrical Home

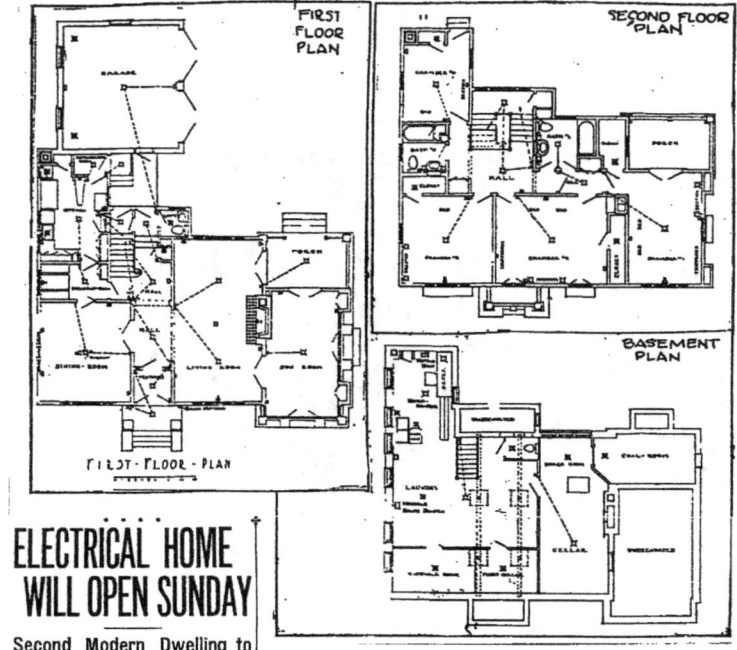

FIRST FLOOR PLAN

SECOND FLOOR PLAN

BASEMENT PLAN

FIRST · FLOOR · PLAN

ELECTRICAL HOME WILL OPEN SUNDAY

Second Modern Dwelling to Attract Many, League Officials Predict.

Cleveland's second modern electrical home, heralded as having even more points of interest to the average Fifth City householder and housekeeper than the first, is scheduled to open for public inspection at 1 Sunday afternoon.

The new home, which is located at 11320 Lake avenue N. W., is to remain open every day from 1 in the afternoon until 10 at night for a month, according to announcement yesterday of the Electrical League, following the completion of practically the last detail of the structure's decoration and furnishing.

The largest crowds that ever inspected an electrically-equipped home is what officials of the league say they expect to visit this "model servantless dwelling."

Lighting fixture workers and a corps of other men will remain at the home until the last minute Saturday, putting each room in order for the four-week's display.

Many months have been spent by the Electrical League, the Residence Wiring Association and the Lighting Fixture Dealers' Society in making the home the finest in electrical labor-saving and illumination equipment ever exhibited in Cleveland.

The home has ninety-five electrical outlets, among which are numerous so-called "convenience" outlets, those used to attach appliances, portable lamps and other devices at will. The structure is equipped with a built-in vacuum cleaner system.

According to household engineers connected with the league, the electrical laundry, in the basement of the home, is the most complete in the city. It includes an electrical washer, ironer, flat iron and clothes dryer—the latter being capable of completely drying a family washing in twenty minutes.

Electrical fire logs in the living room, a master switch controlling the principal lights over the entire home from the master's bed room for emergency purpose, a specially lighted summer roof garden in the rear and model illumination throughout the home are other features of this last word in modern homes.

The league has engaged seven demonstrators to explain every detail of the electrical equipment to visitors. Heads of families will be presented with a booklet containing the electrical plans of the home for use in constructing other homes or in re-wiring older structures.

Admission to this structure, as in the case of the first home, will be free. This home was built for the league by the Phil Marquard Real Estate & Building Co. The furnishings and draperies are being provided by the Young Furniture Co.

"New Lake Ave. Home"

Have you noticed the activity in home building on Lake av. and Edgewater dr. right now? Take your Sunday afternoon ride and see this beautiful, inspiring sight, and mostly all homes built for owners. This convinces the most skeptical where the coming residence location is, and those that have been waiting since the war to decide on their new home, RIGHT NOW is the time before the spring rush and high prices. We invite you to stop and see our new, distinctive tapestry brick home nearing completion at

11400 LAKE AVENUE

Solid tapestry brick, double garage attached; new type architecture, distinctive and a beauty, being so different from other homes; built amongst beautiful trees and shrubbery, with fine view of lake. Open today and during week.

Phil Marquard R. E. & Bldg. Co.

22 Years Home Builders in Greater Cleveland

Sunday—Phone Lakewood 781.
Office Phones—Main 5865-5866—Central 889.

Above left 1922, right 1923 (PD Archives)

The Regnatz Dining Hall

Caroline Obelz Regnatz and her husband Anton immigrated to America from Europe in 1906. According to Cleveland historian and author, Gary Swilik, they were German but soon learned English and went to work. Caroline operated a bakery business and Anton was a brick mason. Mrs. Regnatz started a catering business around 1917 for various churches and other organizations, including a kitchen where she fed the troops free meals before they left Cleveland for the long trip to the European battle front.

It's likely that PH may have met Anton the brick mason in the course of the building business but according to family lore, the Marquard children first came in contact with Mrs. Regnatz when she was running the kitchen at John Carroll University. They frequently came home from school raving about her delicious food. As a result, their father decided to meet her and sample the cuisine. Evidently he loved it, especially her apple pie. Subsequently, he hired her to run the kitchen at his home. She also taught cooking classes to girls at local Catholic high schools. The two families became very close friends. Our old albums contain many photos of the Regnatzes with various members of the Marquard family.

Recognizing Caroline's talent and business sense, an arrangement was made to start a restaurant on Marquard property at 3218 Warren, where the Regnatzes could live and work. The Roseland Dining Hall opened in 1920 and became an immediate sensation and profitable establishment. In 1922 they needed to expand, so PH built a new facility located at 3242 Warren that was nearly ten times the size of Roseland. The new Regnatz Dining Hall could seat 400 and was said to serve up to 1,000 meals daily. Grandfather leased this building to Regnatz with terms that included a small percentage of the gross receipts.

The Marquards had outgrown the ballroom and rathskeller in their home so this new facility was perfect for family wedding receptions and larger gatherings. The children were getting older and going off to school so I think that PH decided to include more of his estate's grounds for the Regnatz operation. He included the fabulous playground with the elaborate slides and swings as well as the sports playing fields and skating rink. The original family playground was located behind and to the left of the mansion. The new facility, refurbished and enlarged for more commercial usage, was moved to the north closer to Regnatz's. The operation was later enhanced with an outdoor summer seating area with umbrella tables amidst the colorful gardens, fish pond and fountains. The old farm windmill, I've been told, pumped water to the restaurant. There was an immensely popular German beer garden and the "Famous Sauerkraut Club." I'm sure the Marquard family loved having all of these perks so close to home!

Since the Pleasant View Theater wasn't getting as much family use, it also was made available to the restaurant for special events. Mrs. Regnatz raised her own chickens and had two or three greenhouses for year-round fresh vegetables and flowers. Overall, Regnatz's had up to nine acres for their usage.

Ted LaBuda

Those greenhouses were in use by the family before the Regnatz operation. Thaddeus "Ted" LaBuda, one of the family groundskeepers was in charge of the greenhouses and later worked with the Regnatzes. After Caroline and Anton passed away, PH leased land to LaBuda in November of 1938, enabling him to start his own retail nursery. The lease agreement included two attached greenhouses and three acres along Warren NW to the intersection of Montrose Road. The lease was for $320 per year with monthly payments of $40.00, except for the months of November, December, January and February, being the off-season.

City directories show Ted and his wife Natalie living and operating the nursery at 3206 Warren. The house has since been torn down.

I remember my father introducing me to Mr. LaBuda back in the fifties when we would go each Spring to buy flowers and vegetable plants. Mr. LaBuda seemed a very nice man who was always happy to see my dad and to reminisce about the good old days.

Regnatz's Demise

According to the Encyclopedia of Cleveland History Regnatz opened two more restaurants in 1931, located on Fairmont at Cedar and at 3618 Euclid Avenue. According to the 1930 U.S. Census the Regnatz family was still renting from PH at 3218 Warren. Actually, the census shows that twenty-three people were living at that address. The grounds included a dormitory for some of the employees, many of whom were teenagers brought over from Germany by Mrs. Regnatz. Gary Swilik also relates how she provided many jobs for disadvantaged kids from the St. Anthony's Boys Home.

In 1936 the amazing Caroline Regnatz died of a brain aneurysm at the age of 55. Her husband, Anton, passed away two years later.

A May 13, 1934 Plain Dealer news story reported that Phil Marquard had leased Regnatz's to Jacob Beck, who apparently was well known in the movie industry, for a five year term with an option to buy for $200,000. Terms included 7% of the gross with a minimum of $300 per month. The lease included seven acres of land as well as the 7,000 square foot main dining room and the several private dining rooms. The new restaurant was scheduled to open Saturday May 19, 1934, under the name "The New Yorker." A new manager, W.J. Jeffries, from California was brought in to run the enterprise. The initial planned entertainment was the Herman Baker Orchestra as well as floor shows. Vin DeCrane recalls the place being called the New Yorker Tavern in the late 1930s.

Gary Swilik's excellent book on Cleveland's West Side historic restaurants tells how the famous dining hall endured under various owners and names, including The

Showboat and the Westwood Inn.

In 1954 the old dining hall along with nine acres was purchased by St. Mary's Romanian Catholic Church for $100,000. The newly constructed church opened in 1960 and Regnatz's was used as the social hall.

I was fortunate to attend more than one wedding in the old cavernous ornate hall back in the 1960s. It was truly a beautiful and quite unique structure. Sadly, the site of a half century of fond memories burned down in July of 1973.

Gary Swilik has authored three volumes of wonderful books on historic restaurants on Cleveland's West Side. Volume I (2010) covers Regnatz's as well as other long-gone Cleveland eateries. These books are available from the West Park Historical Society or directly from Mr. Swilik who may be contacted at gshatterhand@aol.com.

Matchbook

Mr. & Mrs. Regnatz's silver anniversary. L-R Marcus Marquard, Rosina Wise, Caroline & Anton Regnatz, Daisy Marquard & John Marquard Jr.

Rear view of Regnatz's. Below: View from Marquard house, note the birdhouses.

Playground & Biergarten

FORMER REGNATZ PLACE IS LEASED

Will Be "New Yorker" With Change in Policy; Realty Clinic Interesting.

BY JAMES G. MONNETT, JR.

One of the interesting transactions closed the last week was leasing of the former Regnatz dining place, 3242 Warren Road N. W., by Phil Marquard, to new control.

Jacob Beck, for years well known in the motion picture industry, took the place for five years with option for five more and an option to purchase for a reported $200,000. The rental is to be 7 per cent. of gross receipts with minimum guaranty of $300 a month.

The place is being renamed "The New Yorker" and W. J. Jeffries of San Francisco, who also has operated restaurants in Los Angeles and Hollywood, has come east to be the manager.

According to Beck there will be a floor show and Herman Baker's Orchestra has been engaged to play. The opening is tentatively set for next Saturday.

The property consists of more than seven acres of land, improved with a large building which for years has been the scene of large parties and family events. The main dining room contains more than 7,000 square feet and there are several private dining rooms. The grounds are equipped with recreational facilities.

Anthony or Joseph and Caroline Regnatz

Left: 5/13/34 article (PD Archives)

Mrs. Regnatz with Rita & David
Marquard 1926.
Fire destroys former Regnatz
Dining Hall July, 1973

The Big House Gets Bigger

"In its hey-day the house boasted 4 floors, a chapel with real pews and altar, a ballroom, two kitchens, two dining rooms, two living rooms, an office, music room, rathskeller and various suites for married adults"...Dorie Faulhaber

Even though Grandfather Marquard had full access to the Regnatz facilities he decided it was time to further enlarge his mansion. Sometime around 1925 he added on another two-story wing on the northern front of the home. It's my understanding that the existing structure had a ballroom on the second floor but he evidently felt a larger one was needed, "So the 10 children could do their dancing at home," as the January 1926 Don Wooton Plain Dealer caricature quoted PH. He added a larger ballroom on the first floor in this new addition and installed a suite of rooms above it. Perhaps the new ballroom was in anticipation of Verona's upcoming wedding.

"I can't remember any formal dances in the ballroom but I do remember friends of my bachelor uncle, Cleo, teaching us the BIG APPLE to the strains of a fairly professional accordionist. Cleo sure could dance!"...Dorie Faulhaber

It may have been about this time that the music room and a second, more formal dining room, known as "Red Dining Room" were added. The room had heavy red drapes and carpet, hence the name.

"I loved the music room. It was elegant, cool, unused, and furnished with stiff expensive furniture the kind you slid right off of. A forever 'virgin' grand piano was featured in one corner and two other corners were really curtained three-cornered nooks with cushioned seats atop chest-like cupboards that held dozens of smelly old books! ANDY AT ANDOVER, THREE PLEBES AT WEST POINT and TARZAN AND THE JEWELS OF OPAR were a few of the titles. The windows opened out on the wide front veranda. Lovers necking in the sofa swing could be listened to. I listened a lot.

My grandfather had this good friend, Father Cyprian, whose presence was so over-powering that I hid behind the blue velvet drapes in the music room every time I knew I must enter the line-up of priest-greeters."...Dorie Faulhaber

Clare DeCrane remembered the visiting priests more fondly. To her they were like family as there always seemed to be at least a few in attendance for dinner and parties. She reminisced how they would often join in the kids' games. One time they were all playing hide and seek in the house and were unable to locate one of the clergy, until they saw smoke arising from the chimney of the girls' little playhouse. Inside was the priest all crouched down smoking a cigar! Outdoors on summer nights the children would often play "Ghost" a type of hide and seek in the dark. Sometimes the friars would surreptitiously join in, pulling up their hoods on their Franciscan robes and scaring the heck out of the kids!

OUR OWN - By Don Wootton

PHIL H. MARQUARD.

"Yes, I had the dance floor addition built on to the house so the ten children could do their dancing right here at home."

Top left: Big Ben with PH, no wonder Dorie was fearful! Right: Caricature from Plain Dealer. Bottom: 1st floor north wing housed the ballroom.

Note changes to the south wing 2nd floor after ca.1925 additions. Bottom photo shows screened summer porch.

Top: Ballroom. Bottom: A view of the lounge from the ballroom. Photos shot by Cleo shortly before family moved from premises in November of 1942.

Top: Original music room ca. 1918
Middle & bottom: New Music Room and Red Dining
Room added ca. 1925 (photos 1942)

The Rathskeller and Prohibition

The house had a German-style rathskeller constructed in the basement. I'm not sure when this was built but I am certain it was very popular during the Prohibition years of 1920-1933. The low-ceilinged rathskeller had a full bar, tables and beer taps. Family lore has it that there may have been some home brew concocted in that basement labyrinth, as well as some whiskey 'imported' from Canada. Cousin Clare remembers that her uncles used to make hard apple cider out in one of the barns.

My father told a tale about how one or more of the family and friends were hijacked in their truck en route to Warren Road, with a load of illegal spirits. Apparently the hijackers treated them roughly and stole the precious cargo. According to Dad the Marquard sons exacted their revenge. A day or so later they returned to the scene of the crime, late on a moonless night, with the same truck on the same route along, as I recall, Lakeshore or Rocky River Drive. But this time instead of the usual cargo, the back of the covered truck carried a load of Marquard boys. Eventually, the same hijackers appeared and blocked the road forcing their truck to a stop. When the bad guys opened the back, the boys leapt upon them and gave them the beating they deserved. The crooks high-tailed it away on foot. Since the would-be thieves' truck was blocking the road the boys had no choice but to push it off the road, so over the cliff it went!

Getting back to the basement, according to Vin DeCrane there was a commercial grade laundry room as well as a drying room with a very large mangle for pressing everything from clothes to draperies and linens. In one of these subterranean rooms was a large carpeted playroom for the kids which contained lockers for the toys. Then there was the dreaded boiler room that, in the words of the 1943 Cleveland Press story: "There are three heating plants in the basement, two of them being auxiliaries to a large boiler which takes a ton of coal a day to fire, when the whole house is in use." Vin remembered taking his turn shoveling coal on cold nights before an automatic feeder was installed.

Down the corridor from the fruit cellars and the foreboding boiler rooms there was a large toolroom and workshop which was the domain of Mr. John Berkley, known as "The Man" by the household staff and the children. Vin tells me he was a somewhat intimidating fellow who the kids and staff were a bit afraid of due to his gruff manner. However, Mr. Berkley kept the house in working order inside and out. He served not only as the chief engineer but also as head groundskeeper. There was a small apartment house on the estate where Mr. Berkley resided.

Rathskeller (6) -Top L-R: Ginny Weidt (David's fiancé), Dauby, Sarah Jane (Fran's wife), John Arth & Verona
Middle: Rita, Dolly (Dauby's wife), Honey, Mary Jane, Gen Arth
Front: Fran & Vin. Ca. 1942

The Family Dogs

The family always had a number of dogs. Francis, especially, was a dog lover evidenced by the many photos of him with his pets. Clare recalled how Grandpa was always coming home with another dog and presenting it to one of the kids as their own. The larger dogs also served as security for the house.

According to my mother the dogs were let out of their pens at night and had "runs" which they would patrol. She was always afraid to venture out to the back of the house at night for fear of the canines. Don Faulhaber commented to me that there was good reason to be afraid as the dogs had a history of biting more than one of the home's inhabitants. He recalled Uncle "Dick" DeCrane suffering a particularly nasty wound.

Vin DeCrane tells how the dog runs were somewhat elaborate and included a ramp over the garden pergola trellis so they could cross over to the other side of the grounds without straying off to the front of the house or the road. Evidently their kennels were kept up on a platform on the trellis.

After the famous Baby Lindberg kidnapping there was a lot of security paranoia among wealthy and well-known citizens.

"Four or five dogs might be living with us, depending on how careful people were driving in and out. Grandpa had white wooden 'horses' obstructing all the entrances for his grandchildren's safety -- he really worried about us."....Dorie Faulhaber

Top & bottom left: Francis
Top right: Mark
Bottom right: Mark, Vin,
Rita & Fran. Ca. 1927

The family dogs: Prince, Shorty & Duke. Top right shows dog run on top of trellis and bottom photo shows the elaborate trellises. Ca. 1935

The Business Moves West

Near the end of 1924, the Marquard enterprise had outgrown the space on Canal Road and the property was needed for the construction of Cleveland's new Union train station and the skyscraper office complex, the Terminal Tower. Consequently, Grandfather sold the two adjoining buildings, the old A. Teachout Mill, to The Union Terminal Co.

He chose 14737–41 Lorain Road in West Park to relocate his companies. The site was just up the road from his home on Warren. PH purchased three acres of land and on February 8, 1925 he awarded contracts for the new mill and business headquarters. The mill was set back from the road next to a railroad siding to accommodate the importing of lumber and the exporting of the finished product when truck delivery wasn't practical. The structure's first floor contained 40,000 square feet and housed most of the heavy machinery and lumber stock. The second level accommodated another 7000 square feet and was utilized as the paint, finish and hardware departments. I remember "Iggy" the old–timer that ran the hardware section. He was a charming little man forever bent–over at the waist from his many years of installing knobs, hinges etc.

I will never forget the sub–level, which is where I worked in the mid–sixties. It housed a huge iron boiler which was wood–fired for the purpose of burning scrap wood, sawdust and often my eyelashes and hair. The fiery inferno also provided the heat and hot water to the cavernous mill.

The three–story brick headquarters was situated street-side facing Lorain Road. The Marquard offices were on the first floor, the basement contained a walk–in vault and storage space. The upper two floors, not in use by the business, were rented out for apartments and offices.

In the early 1940s the headquarters was sold and the offices were consolidated in the mill itself. The building still stands today with the Marquard name proudly carved in stone near the top. The first floor is now home to Cowan's Bar and the upper floors remain apartments.*

During my time working at the mill, I would run up the black cinder drive to the then Zephyr bar and try to finish a sandwich during the half-hour lunch break. A steam whistle signaled when the break was over and I'd hurry back. One time I was late returning and was chastised by my co-workers. I had no idea how significant that whistle was to them. After that I packed my lunch. Most of my time on the job was spent sweeping and collecting the scraps to feed that giant boiler. I also unloaded and stacked raw lumber from the rail cars. I think I still have some of the splinters as mementos.

*See Epilogue "Vanishing Legacy"

9/14/24 PD Archives

NEW MARQUARD PLANT

Contract is Awarded to Boldt Construction Co.

The Marquard Sash & Door Co. has, through the George S. Rider Co., industrial engineers, awarded contracts for the construction of a new manufacturing plant to the Boldt Construction Co.

The building will be of brick, structural steel and wood construction about 116 by 280 feet and will contain offices, boiler house, dry kilns, manufacturing and storage of finished products, all under one roof.

The new building will be located on the New York Central railroad with access from Lorain avenue, a manufacturing district which is developing quite rapidly.

Top: New Marquard HQ. & 1918 ad

133

.Fire Destroys Old Sash & Door Buildings

On Saturday July 18, 1925 the Cleveland newspapers headlined the spectacular, though tragic, fire at the former Marquard Sash & Door Company (earlier known as the A. Teachout Mill) on Canal Road near West 3rd. The buildings were considered a landmark in the Cleveland Flats. The business suffered a previous fire in 1900.

This latest fire was discovered by the night watchman, Henry Miller. Assistant Fire Chief John Granger believed the fire started in a second floor sawdust chute. All downtown fire companies, as well as the crew of the fire tugboat "John H. Farley" fought the blaze. Before it was over three firemen were injured, one seriously. They were David Andrews who had severe bruises about the head, Bernard McArdle with cuts on the head and face and John Collins who suffered serious internal injuries. Gilbert Turnbull, the tugboat pilot fell overboard but was safely rescued.

The newspapers told of flames leaping a hundred feet in the air. Thousands of feet of soft pine and other wood stock were stored in the buildings. Railroad, automobile and trolley traffic in the area was at a halt and had to be rerouted. Hundreds of onlookers gathered to watch the blaze. Thousands of dollars worth of heavy machinery on the upper levels of the building crashed through the burning floors to the basement below causing the walls to cave in. A 15,000 gallon water tank on the roof boiled over several times and helped keep the flames in check.

Although the buildings had been sold to Union Terminals, Marquard had not yet removed all of his machinery, equipment and stock. Fred Marquard estimated the damage at $150,000.

3 FIREMEN HURT IN $150,000 BLAZE

Flames Raze Building on Flats, Property of Terminals Co.

Three firemen were injured, one perhaps seriously when fire razed the former A. Teachout Co. building on Canal road S. W., near W. 3d street yesterday.

The building, owned by the Union Terminals Co., was to have been torn down to make way for the new Union depot. The building was occupied by the Marquard Sash & Door Co.

Bernard McArdle, 29, 15801 Bernice avenue S. W.; John Collins, 29, 3305 W. 33d street and David Andrews, 23, 3445 W. 125th street were the firemen injured. They were struck by the nozzle of a high pressure hose which squirmed out of their grasp. All were taken to Charity hospital. McArdle had a fractured jaw, Andrews was bruised. Collins, with possible internal injuries, was the most seriously injured.

A 15,000-gallon water tank atop the building boiled over several times and checked the flames. Loss was estimated at $150,000.

TUG BATTLES BLAZE

Burning of the A. Teachout building on Canal-rd while downtown fire companies battled the spectacular blaze from Canal-rd, the crew of the fire tug Farley struggled to force the tottering walls inward, to prevent demoralization of the B. & O. railroad which lies between the building and the river. The building was occupied by the Marquard Sash and Door Co.

Verona's Lavish Wedding

On Thursday morning January 21, 1926, Phil Marquard's eldest daughter Verona was married to Alfred C. DeCrane at St. Stephen's Church on West 54th, in what can only be called an elaborate affair. The Arizona Observer newspaper described it as "The most important event in Catholic circles in a long time." Cleveland's Archbishop Joseph Schrembs officiated with over 28 local and out of town priests and deacons in attendance, including the Right Reverend Michael J. Gallagher, Bishop of Detroit. The bride and groom had no fewer than 17 wedding attendants. The sanctuary was made a bower of ferns and flowers and the church was filled to overflow capacity. Music was provided by Professor John Menth's male choir and a string orchestra. The ceremony was a solemn pontifical nuptial Mass. Archbishop Schrembs dedicated it to Verona's late beloved mother Sophia whom he described as "a splendid example of a wife and mother."

After pushing through the crowd of hundreds of invitees and curious bystanders outside the church, the long wedding procession, escorted by many Cleveland police cars, made its way to the Regnatz Dining Hall which served breakfast for 300. The reception took place both at the Big House as well as Regnatz's. I'm guessing that the ball room dance floor was put to good use that evening. It was well known that the Marquards loved a good party and money was not a problem for the family during the Roaring Twenties.

When the couple returned from their Arizona and California honeymoon they had a beautiful new home awaiting them on the north side of the mansion at 3256 Warren. Pa presented it to them as a wedding present. The substantial home was built of brick and stucco with a clay tile roof, designed in the Southwestern or Spanish style.

Verona and Al DeCrane's first child, Vincent, nicknamed

"Sonny," was born on August 27, 1927, providing PH with the first of many grandchildren.

Top: left Cleo, middle Al DeCrane, Roland, Philip, Wilfred. Bottom left David, Rita front left, 4th from left Honey, Francis in between Honey & Verona.

Miss Verona Marquard Married With Brilliant Ceremony At St. Stephen's Church In Cleveland Last Thursday

Phoenix society will read with much interest of the marriage of Miss Verona Marquard, daughter of Philip H. Marquard, of Cleveland, Ohio, and formerly a winter resident of this city, to Alfred Charles DeCrane, which took place last week at St. Stephen's church, in Cleveland, Mr. and Mrs. DeCrane are spending a part of their honeymoon in Phoenix, where they are being entertained extensively by the many friends of the former Miss Marquard.

The following is the story of the wedding appearing in the Cleveland News:

One of the most colorful weddings of the season was solemnized Thursday morning in St. Joseph's church, when Miss Verona I. Marquard, daughter of Philip H. Marquard, 2260 Warren road, became the bride of Alfred C. DeCrane, son of Mr. and Mrs. Peter J. DeCrane, of 2195 Clark avenue.

Rt. Rev. Joseph Schrembs, bishop of Cleveland, officiated at the marriage service, assisted by Rt. Rev. Msgr. Nicholas Pfeil, Msgr. Francis Moran, Msgr. Peter M. Cerny and visiting priests in the sanctuary. Tall baskets of roses and southern lilies adorned the altar, which was lighted with cathedral candles. The front pews were marked by white ribbons and bouquets of sweet peas. The wedding music was furnished by St. John A. Meeth's male choir and string orchestra.

The bride, escorted to the altar and given in marriage by her father, was lovely in her wedding gown of white wedding ring velvet, fashioned with flowing long sleeves and a gauzy tip and studded with rhinestones. A duchesse lace veil was arranged with a bandeau of lace and pearls.

and she carried a shower bouquet of Ophelia roses and lilies of the valley.

Miss Olivia Marquard attended her sister as maid of honor, wearing a gold lace gown, a hat of gold lace, trimmed with orchid streamers, and carrying an arm bouquet of Coolidge roses and orchid colored sweet peas.

The five bridesmaids were similar models of satin in pastel shades, hats to match and carried arm bouquets. The bridesmaids included Miss Evelyn Marquard, cousin of the bride, wearing light blue satin, trimmed with silver cloth and lace, a hat of blue malina trimmed with rhinestones and pale green streamers. She carried Premet roses. Frances Wasmer, in pale green satin, a pale green malina hat trimmed with rhinestones and pink streamers and carrying Ophelia roses, and Mildred Riley, in orchid satin, an orchid maline hat trimmed with rhinestones and pale green streamers. She carried Calvin Coolidge roses.

The flower girls included the Misses Rita Marquard, sister of the bride, wearing a pale blue georgette frock ruffled with lace; Marie DeCrane, sister of the bridegroom, in pink georgette and lace, and Constance Marquard, cousin of the bride, in yellow georgette and lace. They carried small baskets filled with rose petals. David Marquard, brother of the bride, served as ring-bearer. Richard

Marquard, cousin of the bride, was herald, and Francis Marquard, brother of the bride, was train bearer.

Mr. DeCrane was attended by his brother, Frank DeCrane, as best man. The ushers included Messrs. Martin DeCrane, Cleo Marquard, brother of the bride; Philip H. Marquard, Jr., brother of the bride; Wilfred Marquard, cousin of the bride, and Roland Marquard, cousin of the bride.

Bishop Michael Gallagher, of Detroit, was included among the visiting clergy from out of the city, others being Rev. William Custer, of Vermillion, O.; Rev. George Shuber and Rev. Charles Reichlin, of Lorain, and Rev. Frank Boyeko, of Baltimore, Md.

Bishop Schrembs, the celebrant of the mass, was assisted by Rev. Joseph Gerz and Rev. Father Linus, O. F. M., deacon and subdeacon, respectively; Rev. Peter Hyland and Rev. Father Cyprian, O. F. M., deacons; Rev. August M. Hackert, S. J., assistant priest, and Very Rev. James A. McFadden, master of ceremonies.

Other priests present at the ceremony were Msgr. Francis T. Moran, D. D., Msgr. Nicholas Pfeil, D. D., and Msgr. Peter Cerveny, D. D., and Rev. E. J. Ahern, Rev. J. M. Rohmer, Rev. Francis Stanton, Rev. John Kinney, Rev. J. J. Schmitt, Rev. Anthony La Battes, Rev. James Heffernan, Rev. Richard Patterson, Rev. Thomas McKinney, Rev. Augustine Thomsick, Rev. Adolph Bieholzer, Rev. J. J. Culnan, Rev. C. H. LeBlonde, Rev. James D. Leahy and Rev. Francis Matthew, O. F. M.

Both the Marquard residence, where the reception was held, and the Regnatz, on Warren road, were elab-

orately decorated with flowers.

Assisting members of the bridal party in receiving at the Marquard home were Mr. and Mrs. Fred Marquard. Mrs. Marquard wearing a handsome gown of pale green and gold lace, a small hat of green and gold; also Mr. and Mrs. John Marquard, the latter wearing blue chiffon over silver, a large black maline hat, and Mr. and Mrs. Joseph Marquard, Mrs. Marquard wearing rose embroidered with steel beads.

The stairway in the reception hall was embanked about with tall baskets of roses, bodies and ferns. Southern smilax festooned the stair railing. Bowls of roses, calendulas, bodies and ferns adorned the tables in the living and dining rooms.

Following the reception the bridal party and guests passed through the canopy from the Marquard home to Regnatz, where the wedding breakfast was served.

The bride's table, centered with a large wedding cake, was lovely with pink roses and tall pink tapers tied with ribbons and clusters of ferns. The other tables, where about 200 guests were served, were attractive with bowls of roses and lilies and tall pink tapers. Boutonnieres of sweet peas, lilies and maidenhair ferns were at each place. The chandeliers and columns in the banquet hall were profusely festooned with southern smilax.

On their return to Cleveland, Mr. DeCrane and his bride will occupy their new home, at 2256 Warren road, Cleveland. The bride is a graduate of Lourdes academy.

Goes to West Coast for Her Honeymoon

MRS. ALFRED C. DeCRANE
B.A. MARQUARD PHOTO

The marriage of Miss Verona I. Marquard, daughter of Mr. Philip H. Marquard, of Lakewood, to Mr. Alfred C. DeCrane, son of Mr. and Mrs. Peter DeCrane, Clark avenue S. W., was an elaborate affair of Jan. 21. Mr. and Mrs DeCrane have left for California on their honeymoon. Bishop Schre...u.celebrant of their nuptial mass at St. Stephen's church.

The "Wedding Present" house at 3256 Warren. Top: south side, bottom: front facing east.

138

Spring Break 1926

After completing the business move to West Park and Verona's wedding Grandfather found time for a spring break. He chose the newest fashionable hotel in Palm Beach, Florida, The Royal Daneli. Palm Beach was the playground for the rich and famous from around the world ever since Henry Flagler developed it and brought the train tracks right to the door of his famous hostelry, The Breakers. Both the Breakers and the Royal Ponciana suffered fires in 1925 and had not yet reopened. Those two landmarks were also considered Victorian and outdated while the Daneli was the latest rage. According to an April 1926 society column in the Plain Dealer, PH's traveling party included his daughter Olivia, his brother John with wife Gertrude, Mr. & Mrs. James C. Marquard, Mrs. Caroline Regnatz and Dorothy Marquard. I think the article contained a typo and that it was actually brother Joseph C. not James C. who was on that trip.

Years later the Daneli became the Mayflower and then the Palm Beach Spa Hotel which was razed in 1983. The Marquards loved to travel, not only throughout the United States but also to Europe. Closer to home the family loved to spend summer days on Lake Erie in the Vermillion area.

Olivia's Wedding

On Wednesday June 20, 1928 at 10AM the second Marquard daughter, Olivia (Honey), married Edwin F. Faulhaber in a ceremony every bit as lavish as Verona's. The rituals took place at St. Mary's Catholic Church at West 30th and Carroll Avenue in Cleveland.

Bishop Schrembs officiated with Bishop Gallagher of Detroit who flew in for the occasion. The pilot of Gallagher's private airplane buzzed the church several times at treetop level wowing the crowd of hundreds of guests and onlookers. There were four Monsignors and more than twenty other pastors and priests assisting the Bishop during the nuptial Mass. Also in attendance was Bishop Dumbowski, who was visiting from Poland.

I have watched home movies of the wedding and reception and can say it was quite a spectacle. The movie is very special since narration was added to it years later by the bride. The crowd outside the church and the police escort of the wedding entourage on the trip back to the family home looks like something from a Hollywood premier. This celebration included up to 400 for breakfast at Regnatz's with the reception at the Big House.

The bride and groom honeymooned on the St. Lawrence River and returned to live for awhile at the Big House and later occupied the Wedding Present House at 3256 Warren after the DeCranes settled in the suite over the ballroom in the Big House. In 1929 Doris Jean was the first of five children born to the loving couple.

"He had lost Grandma and his eldest son before I arrived to share the house with my parents, my twin brothers, seven young uncles, two aunts, some in-laws and three young cousins.......it was no trick for grandpa to just keep adding on to THE BIG HOUSE."...Dorie Faulhaber

BISHOP OFFICIATES AT MARRIAGE RITE

Miss Marquard Becomes Bride of Edwin F. Faulhaber

The wedding of Miss Olivia Gertrude Marquard, daughter of Philip H. Marquard, 3260 Warren rd., and Edwin Francis Faulhaber, son of Mr. and Mrs. George Faulhaber, 2206 West blvd., took place in St. Mary's church at ten Wednesday morning, with the Rt. Rev. Joseph Schrembs, D.D., Bishop of Cleveland, as celebrant of the nuptial Mass and witness to their vows.

The presence of the Rt. Rev. Michael J. Gallagher, D.D., Bishop of Detroit, several of the monsignori of the Cleveland diocese and a number of priests of local parishes added an impressive dignity to the service.

The interior of the church had been turned over to decorators since Tuesday afternoon and the interior was a mass of floral decorations.

Crowd Outside Church

Large crowds in W. 30th st., in the vicinity of the church manifested their interest in the occasion. These remained throughout the ceremony, viewing with special interest the procession of the bridal party, the two Bishops and the other clergy from the parlors of the Carroll university building across the street to the church.

The Rt. Rev. Msgr. Joseph P. Smith, V.G., LL.D., P.A., was the assistant priest at the celebration of the Pontifical Nuptial Mass and the Rev. Lucas Keenemund, O.F.M., pastor of Our Lady of the Angels parish, and the Rev. E. J. Zurlinden, S.J., Canisge, were the deacon and subdeacon.

The Rt. Rev. Msgr. James A. Mc-Fadden, chancellor, and the Rt. Rev. Msgr. Nicholas Pfeil, pastor of St. Peter's parish, were the deacons of honor to the Bishop of Cleveland, and the Rev. Francis J. Stanton, pastor of St. Angela's parish, Fairview village, and the Rev. John R. Kenny, pastor of St. Colman's parish, were the chaplains to Bishop Gallagher.

The bridal party, including the several young men and young women attendants and the ushers, received Holy Communion.

Bishop Outlines Marriage Ideals

The address of the Rt. Rev. Bishop outlined the beauty of the Catholic wedding and the purpose of God in instituting the union of man and woman.

"It is the most sacred relation between man and woman," he said, "and it is ordained for a high and holy purpose. In the Church we see its beauty exemplified on an occasion of this kind and the Church, through her bishop, calls down upon the newly married couple every blessing that their new relation may continue through a happy, peaceful and protracted span of years.

"It is the teaching of the Church, the Bishop said, that whatever vicissitudes may come to the married couple, the graces that flow from the Sacrament of Matrimony serve to strengthen and encourage them.

Bishop again referred to current thought on marriage, saying that life is diametrically opposed to

Many Priests Present

These other priests were in the sanctuary: The Revs. A. M. Hackett, S.J., pastor of St. Mary's parish; George N. Habig, diocesan secretary; T. J. Smith, S.J., of John Carroll university; James Heffernan, pastor of St. Luke's parish; Richard J. Patterson, pastor of St. Christopher's; Thomas E. McKenney, pastor of Our Lady of the Blessed Sacrament parish; Edward A. Kirby, D.D., pastor of St. Cecilia's parish; M. D. Leahy, pastor of St. James' parish; Polycarp Rhode, O.F.M., of the Franciscan monastery, Rocky River drive; S. J. Kreusch, C.PP.S., pastor of Our Lady of Good Counsel parish; George Reber, pastor of St. Boniface's parish; John Treacy, assistant at St. Luke's church.

The Revs. Murtha Boylan, S.J., rector of John Carroll university; F. A. Moeller, S.J., of St. Mary's parish; P. X. Heiermann, S.J., of St. Mary's parish; Joseph J. Schmitt, pastor of St. Clement's parish; Sante Gattuso, O.D.M., pastor of St. Rocco's parish.

The Revs. Joseph J. Mullen, D.D., Ph.D., of Our Lady of the Lake seminary; Matthew Schmitz, O.F.M., superior of the Franciscan monastery; E. J. Ahern, chaplain at St. John's hospital; George N. Stuber, pastor of St. Mary's parish, Bedford, and Charles Belden, V.F., pastor of St. Joseph's parish, Lorain.

After the church service dinner was served at Regnatz inn to 300 guests,

Gives Daughter in Marriage

Picture shows Philip H. Marquard escorting his daughter Olivia Gertrude into St. Mary's church, where Miss Marquard became the bride of Edwin Francis Faulhaber, Wednesday morning.

MISS MARQUARD IS FAULHABER BRIDE

West Siders Married in Brilliant Ceremony at St. Mary's.

(Photo on Picture Page)

With all the pomp and color and ceremony of the Catholic church, with the scarlet of bishops' robes and the fragrance of incense, the marriage of Miss Olivia Gertrude Marquard, daughter of Phil H. Marquard, 3260 Warren Road N. W., and Edwin Francis Faulhaber, son of Mr. and Mrs. George E. Faulhaber, 2206 West Boulevard S. W., was celebrated yesterday morning at St. Mary's Catholic Church, W. 30th Street and Carroll Avenue N. W.

Bishop Joseph Schrembs, in his high gold mitre and his brocaded vestments, bearing the gold crozier that signifies his office as shepherd of his people, officiated at the nuptial mass and witnessed the vows. Also in the processional that followed the bridal couple into the church were Bishop Michael J. Gallagher of the Diocese of Detroit, four monsignori and more than a score of assisting priests.

Throng at Church Door.

Hundreds of onlookers, anxious to get a peep at the bridal party, filled the sidewalks and pressed close to the green awning under which the guests passed into the church. Over their heads an airplane soared, swooping down almost to the tree tops. The plane was waiting to take Bishop Gallagher back to Detroit.

First in the processional came the tiny herald, Philip Battes, with yellow hair and a black satin suit. Then came the eleven ushers, and the six senior bridesmaids, in gold shot taffeta and gold horsehair hats.

Junior Bridesmaids.

Six tiny junior bridesmaids, also in gold taffeta, were next, then the maid of honor, Miss Evelyn Marquard, cousin of the bride, dressed in daffodil yellow taffeta trimmed with green, and the matron of honor, Mrs. Alfred C. DeCrane, sister of the bride, in green taffeta. Flower girls and ring bearer preceded the bride, who entered on the arm of her father. She wore a Corbeau model gown in ivory white taffeta with a veil of real lace and an ivory tinted tulle train. She carried a bouquet of lilies of the valley.

The church gleamed with tapers and pink and white peonies, and blue delphinium entwined with southern smilax were the decorations.

More than 300 attended the wedding breakfast at Regnatz's after the ceremony.

Top row Clara Schraeder Dorothy Mehr Evelyn Marquard David Marquard Valerie Marquard Catherine
next row Rita Marquard, Betty Marquard Mary Eugenia Marquard, Philip Pochart Helen
continued The bride Stoney Marquard Gene Bleckheiser Phil Boller Rita Connie Marquard
Gene

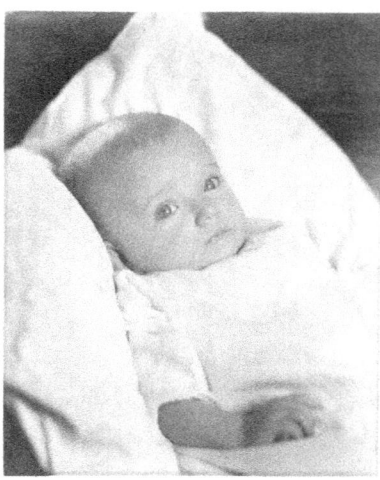

Doris Jean Faulhaber born on
8/14/1929

Family photo taken in Music Room ca. 1931. Standing L-R: Vincent, David, Mark, Fran, Cleo, Adelbert, Al DeCrane, Philip, Ed Faulhaber
Sitting L-R: Rita, Vin DeCrane, Doris Faulhaber, Phil H., Clarice, Verona holding Al DeCrane Jr., Olivia holding twins Donald & David.
Below: Verona & Honey ca. 1922

Clockwise: Clarice, & Vin DeCrane with Dorie. Dorie, Vin & Clarice at the Blessed Virgin shrine on the estate. Vin & Clarice. Ca. 1930

The College Years

Phil and Sophia's brood was gradually going their own way, but the Big House and the tight-knit family seemed to constantly call them back. The oldest girls were now married yet still lived at or near 3260 Warren. Often when the kids left home for more than a short time, their pa and much of the family would take to the road to visit them.

Most, if not all of the boys attended St. Ignatius High School and then enrolled and graduated from John Carroll University in Cleveland. Clare told me how her mother Verona, who was very bright, regretted not being able to attend college as Pa had said that he really needed her around to supervise and help with the younger children and the running of the household. Her brothers often would lovingly refer to her as "Mother Superior."

In 1926 Marcus heard his calling and enrolled at St. Joseph's Franciscan Seminary at Mayslake in Hinsdale, Illinois, embarking on his long road to the priesthood. He was 14 years old when he left home. The family visited him frequently and later accompanied him when he sailed off to Europe to continue his studies. The trip turned into a grand tour of the continent, which naturally included a contingent of priests and visits to dozens of holy sites. He was ordained Fr. Philip in 1939. (Just what we needed another Philip!) I'm sure that had to be his Pa's proudest moment.

In 1928 Philip Frederick left John Carroll to attend Georgetown Law School in Washington D.C. Cleo also attended Georgetown. This of course prompted another family sojourn to our nation's capitol, where the family took in all of the historic sights and monuments, including a tour of the White House. In 1932 Phil Jr. graduated second in his class, received his L.L.B degree and passed the Ohio State Bar examination. From

1932–33 he was enrolled at the Harvard School of Business in Cambridge, Massachusetts. Later, Georgetown awarded my father his Doctorate of Law degree (JD).

"In Uncle Phil's room, there were pictures inscribed "To Phil--with all my love and kisses." Uncle Phil, the second oldest uncle, was so handsome he was often told by his irrepressible brothers that he was prettier than his girlfriends. Uncle Phil was the fussiest about his possessions, but as long as we didn't touch his law books or step through his top hat, his temper was no problem and his generosity continued. He always had an extra buck for his younger brothers and a doll or toy for us kids."...Dorie Faulhaber

At that time Dad did have somewhat of a reputation as a playboy.

Phil (1934) & Dauby (1929) in their
St. Ignatius sweaters

JAN. 6 / 1929

Top L-R: Fran in his John Carroll
dorm room, Mark, Verona ?, PH,
Philip & Cleo in Washington D.C.
Bottom: Mark the Novice and Dauby
the football hero.

L-R top-: In DC, David, PH,
Vin, ?, Cleo. Next: PH, ?, Philip,
Cleo. Below: Mark at St. Peter's.
Vin & Al DeCrane(?) in Rome.

"In my Father's House there are many rooms" (John 14:2)

Money was not an issue for PH in the 1920s as evidenced by his generous charitable donations, the resplendent weddings and the ever–enlarging mansion. The house had grown to up to 60 rooms and over 16,000 square feet of floorspace. I wondered how that compared to other grand homes of the day.

The largest mansions in Cleveland were on Euclid Avenue's "Millionaires Row." The biggest of these homes was the Samuel Mather mansion that was built in 1910, having 45 rooms. The infamous Franklin Castle in Cleveland has 20 rooms.

Detroit's largest mansion was built by the Fisher auto body family in 1925 for Bishop Gallagher's residence. It is 68 rooms and over 30,000 square feet. Perhaps the Bishop was inspired by the Marquard Mansion, which he had often visited. In 1926 Henry Ford built his Fairlane mansion which has 56 rooms. My father reminisced one time how the family visited Thomas Jefferson's Monticello and after the tour, much to the adults' embarrassment, one of the kids commented that their house was larger. Monticello has 43 rooms and is 11,000 square feet. Of course, it is difficult to compare the interior of houses due to the various ways the rooms and square footage are counted and measured.

Cousin Clare recalled when she was a young teen there weren't many neighbor boys her age. One day at the nearby skating rink she met one she liked. He asked if he might visit at her home. She readily agreed, only to have him admit that he was very puzzled as to which of the many doors to the large house he should come to? Clare gave him careful directions to the side-door of the servants' kitchen. She explained that the cook or maid would admit him and send for her. Possibly she didn't care to have him come to the main entrance to endure the scrutiny of her uncles and parents.

PH certainly had the money and the means to build an impressive and luxurious residence as was the custom of egocentric millionaires of the times. However, he is described, by most, as a practical and sensible man especially when it came to his children and personal life. Although the house was stately, it was tasteful and not overly ostentatious. It's noteworthy how the house was screened from the road by large trees and plantings. Probably not a design chosen by an egotistical person.

"Our family always had thrifty peasant ways even when Grandpa's bankroll was royal!"....Dorie Faulhaber

Cleveland Press photo 1943

Trees and shrubs shroud the house. Note the
sky apartment in the bottom photo.

Top: from foyer facing living room and music room
beyond.
Bottom: Central staircase from foyer 1942

Front living room 1942

Artwork and Christmas

"I remember much of those early years...we lived in my maternal Grandfather's house; THE BIG HOUSE. I loved all sixty rooms of it, every piece of furniture, the junk and the treasures, even the heavy, gilt-framed, oozy oils depicting scenes of highly unlikely pastoral activities. For example a shepherd boy holding a mammoth cucumber."...Dorie Faulhaber

Much of the artwork in the home were religious paintings and statuary. According to my father, PH commissioned Catholic nuns in France to complete many of the paintings. Those paintings were done in oils on tapestry. Some of the paintings were not overtly religious but depicted stories or lessons for children. Two of those hung on our home's walls. One was probably three and a half foot high and four foot wide with a huge gold-gilded rococo frame. As I recall it showed a boy sleeping under a tree near the water's edge with two or three other children whispering, with a pail of water, apparently plotting to douse the lazy boy. One painting, which I now have, is of a shepherd boy on a mountain ledge holding a black lamb which he had apparently rescued. It's over two feet wide and more than three feet tall, also with a gold frame.

Closing out 1928 and ringing in 1929 Grandfather put his ballroom to good use by hosting a dinner dance with Christmas entertainment according to the January 6, 1929 Plain Dealer society page. The party was to announce the engagement of Fred and Laura's daughter Evelyn Sophia who was to marry Anthony Schwind.

Another joyous occasion in 1929 was the birth of Clarice Sophia, Al and Verona's second child. Clare, now a widow residing in California, told me recently how Grandfather would often take her with him to attend his daily Mass at the Poor Clare's convent chapel. When Clare's husband, Ed Walsh, passed away in 1971 she called the Poor Clares from California to request prayers for him. The elderly nun who answered the phone remembered her and introduced herself as Sister Clarice. She said Clare was named after her! She had never known why the name was chosen for her. Her middle name of course was to honor her grandmother. The older generation names seem to be making a comeback; in 2014 Sophia was the most popular name for girls while Olivia ranked third.

Grandfather loved the Christmas season and always bedecked the house and grounds with yuletide decorations. From the old photos one can see a virtual forest of Christmas trees in and around the house as well as pine and holly bunting covering the entranceway and anywhere else that they could adhere the decorations. I'm amazed that there was never a disastrous fire. There was however a gas explosion in 1932 that propelled a lead pipe up from the basement through the upper floors that came very close to striking three-year old Clarice and a housemaid, Agnes Macejko.

PH was always certain to see to the kids' needs which included toys and entertainment. While touring the house in 2010 Vin DeCrane recalled how the third floor of the house had large-gauge model train tracks running along the baseboards with holes cut through them at certain points so the train could pass between rooms. The trains were also a big attraction in the ballroom's Christmas display. Vin thought the train buff was our Uncle Vincent Marquard (or Beanie as he was nicknamed). He thought Uncle Vin recovered those trains years later for his children. However he was unable to find parts for the old train collection so he traded them in for a more modern set.

"The ballroom was a large many-windowed room....with a shiny but strongly marked floor that had withstood the ravages of many little tricycle wheels, roller skate exhibitions and electric train displays. The train was used in the huge Christmas display we all loved so. Twelve or more tall evergreen trees would be placed at either end of the room framing an over-sized Nativity scene. The train wound in and out of the whole business often getting derailed at the most inaccessible spot. My uncles who were in charge had us kids well-trained--not to touch anything!

Piles of Christmas presents were waiting for us there when Santa Claus (usually played by my Uncle Dauby) arrived. We knew it was our large, sweet, rough-housing uncle sweating under the red suit and beard, but he loved his role so much that we also knew it would be really stinky of us to spoil his fun.".... Dorie Faulhaber

My father inherited this love for Yuletide bunting and always made sure our home was covered in pine boughs. He also liked to buy live fir trees with the root balls in large buckets, which served as the stand and weighed a ton. At first thaw he would plant the trees in our yard. Some survive to this day and are over 40 feet tall.

DEC. 25 / 1928

DEC. 25 1928

Prev. Pg: Christmas in the ballroom.
Top: Big House adorned for holidays
Bottom: Fred's house also decked out
L-R: Philip, John or PH, Dickie, Fred, David & Mark.
Not sure of the clock's significance.

Foyer and living room fireplace 1942

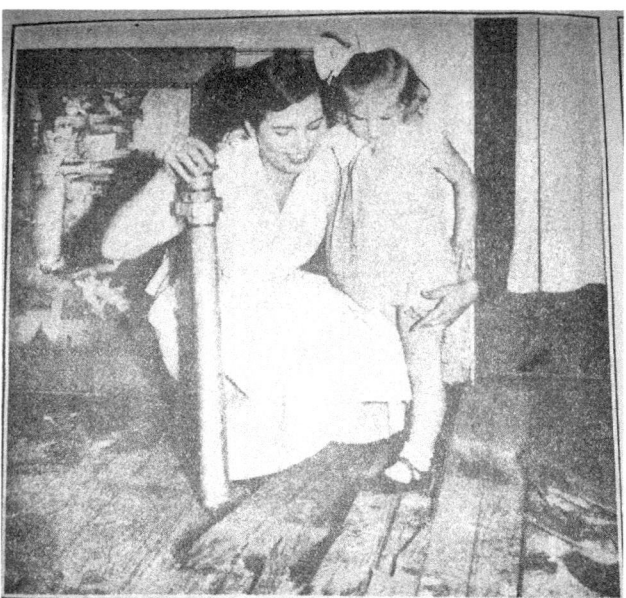

EXPLOSION. A piece of lead pipe narrowly missed striking three-year-old Clarice De Crane and Agnes Macefks, housemaid, when a gas explosion occurred in the Phil H. Marquard residence, 3260 Warren Road N. W., late yesterday afternoon. Clarice is Marquard's granddaughter.

21 PERILED, BLAST HURLS PIPE IN HOME

Leaking Gas Ignited in 50-Room West Side House.

A gas explosion in the basement of the home of Phil H. Marquard, 3260 Warren Road N. W., late yesterday afternoon damaged the sewing room on the first floor of the 50-room residence. Clarice De Crane, Marquard's three-year-old granddaughter, and Agnes Macejko, a maid employed in the home, narrowly escaped injury.

Several feet of four-inch lead pipe tore through the floor boards, severing electric wires, and hit the ceiling, denting the surface. The maid was leading Clarice through the room, when the pipe whizzed past, narrowly missing the child's head.

Marquard is the father of twelve children. His daughter, Mrs. A. C. De Crane, who lives with him, is the mother of four. Including employes, there are 22 in the household.

All but one had gathered for dinner in the summer dining room, which opens directly from the sewing room.

Alarm reigned until Vincent Marquard, eighteen-year-old son, was found. He had been in the basement installing a new hot water boiler, and it was thought he was still downstairs when the explosion occurred. He strolled into the house from the ten-acre grounds shortly afterward and relieved the family's anxiety.

According to Battalion Fire Chief John Sterling, the plumbing work being done in the basement started a gas leak. An ignited hot water heater near-by set off the accumulated gas. No fire resulted. Damage was estimated at about $500.

Marquard is president of the Phil Marquard Real Estate & Building Co. and of the Marquard Sash & Door Manufacturing Co., 14737 Lorain Avenue.

Closing Out the Decade

The Twenties were certainly the heyday for the family as well as for Cleveland and the country as a whole. Many honors were bestowed on Phil H. Marquard, and his businesses and family were doing better than ever. New home subdivisions continued to be innovative and classical all at once. The 1928 Greenwood–Daleview subdivision in the Lakewood Heights section featured "Homes Beautiful" of Spanish, English Tudor and American Colonial architecture.

THIS MARBLE STATUE of the Virgin and Child was recently put in place above the main entrance to St. Mary's seminary on Ansel road N. E. Smaller statues of St. Charles Borromeo and St. Thomas Aquinas will be placed in niches at either side of the door. The statues, made in Germany, are the gift of Philip Marquard and family.

1928.

Cents Per Copy

Phil. H. Marquard Made Knight Of Saint Gregory By Pope Pius

CLEVELAND, Ohio, April 20—Gold and scarlet badges and glistening swords, insignia of the rank of knight commander of the Order of St. Gregory the Great, were bestowed on three Clevelanders Thursday night at ancient and impressive ceremonies in St. John's Cathedral.

The three kneeling before Bishop Joseph Schrembs, seated at the high altar, received the marks of their rank in the presence of dignitaries of the church and a full congregation of laymen, representative of all walks of the city's life.

John J. Bernet, Anthony Carlin and Philip Marquard, were the recipients of the distinctive honor of membership in the order founded 97 years ago by Pope Gregory XVI to honor Catholic laymen in the name of his predecessor of the early church, the greatest of the Gregories.

Opens With Procession

The ceremonies opened with a procession that moved through the aisles of the church while a choir directed by Rev. James J. Duffy, chanted hyms.

In the procession marched priests in cassock and surplice, half a dozen Franciscan monks in their brown habits, several monsignori in purple. Bishop Schrembs, attended by three knight commanders and the three to be created, closed the procession.

When the bishop had seated himself on the throne, his attendants grouped about him, Msgr. James A. McFadden, chancellor of the Cleveland diocese, ascended the pulpit and read the papal briefs citing the three for meritorious charitable work.

Note of Sadness

A note of sadness crept into the ceremonies as Bishop Schrembs revealed that Martin O'Neil of Akron was to have been among those honored, but his untimely death last fall came before the honor could be bestowed upon him.

As the ceremonies proceeded, the bishop called each of the three before him and striking the left shoulder of each with a sword invoked the blessing of God, then blessing the sword, he handed it to the knight with the words:

"Receive the sword of the order May it be a symbol of your loyalty to your church.'

He next pinned the octagonal cross of gold surfaced with red and with a likeness of St. Gregory the Great in the center about the necks of Bernet, Carlin and Marquard.

Top: Cleveland Stadium PH 2nd
from right
Right: PH in center at Regnatz's

The shrine was originally on south side of house. Note halo of electric lights. Photo on left shows it encased in glass after donation to Poor Clare's Monastery in 1942.

THE CATHOLIC UNIVERSE BULLETIN

Real Estate Head, Type of Home He Is Building

Phil Marquard and One of His "Homes Beautiful"

Phil H. Marquard, president of the Phil Marquard Real Estate & Building Co., Cleveland's oldest builders of "Homes Beautiful," established 40 years ago, announces that his company will improve 26 exclusive homesites off Rocky River dr., on Greenwood ave., between St. Joseph's academy and the parish school of Our Lady of Angels, and on Daleview ave., between Madison and Hilliard rd.

These homesites are highly restricted and the Phil Marquard Real Estate & Building Co. has now completed the first four brick homes of 5, 7, and 8 rooms in English and Spanish architecture, with variegated shingled roofs and solid brick two-car garage. The Marquard company is now drawing plans for homes costing as low as $16,500.

Many of the lots are heavily wooded with oak, birch, and pine trees. They are conveniently located near the new 80-foot Rocky River blvd., overlooking the Metropolitan Parkway, the Metropolitan Golf course, the Convent of the Poor Clares, St. Joseph's academy, and Our Lady of the Angels' church and school. Marquard claims that these homes will be the last word in moderate priced homes, and invites the public to inspect them. They are open daily from 9 to 9 p. m. Private appointment may be made by calling Lakewood 9540.

Within short walking distance there are a shopping center, banks, picture homes, and a bus line operating off Rocky River dr., connecting with Clifton blvd., Detroit, Madison, and Lorain ave. cars.

For many years people have been waiting for the development of these two beautiful properties and they are now buying homesites and permanent homes in these new developments which are the finest off Rocky River dr. Buyers can feel satisfied that they have fully provided for their children's safety and conveniences as there are no car tracks to cross, no more worries for mothers in this location. Special introductory prices and terms are being offered to the first buyers.

HALF MILLION GOES INTO NEW HOUSES

Marquard Co. Buys 52 Kleinman Sites for Improvement.

BY JAMES G. MONNETT, JR.

One of the largest developments of moderate priced homes in several years was announced yesterday when the Marquard Real Estate & Building Co. closed negotiations for purchase of the sites from the S. H. Kleinman Realty Co., National City building.

Fifty-two lots in the section bounded by Warren road, Riverside drive, Lorain avenue and Munn road were taken by the Marquard company at around $125,000.

The houses to be constructed will range in building cost from $7,500 to $15,000 each. The total will be more than $500,000. Construction will be started immediately following completion of paving of several streets which now is in progress, Munn road being almost finished. Each house will be of distinct exterior design. The group will include Dutch and New England colonials, California bungalows and French small chateau type, while all will contain features for which the Marquard organization has been noted.

This is the initial step in building moderate priced homes by the Marquard Co. and is in response to a heavy demand, according to Phil H. Marquard, president. The company has been engaged for a quarter century in building homes of much greater cost in Lakewood and Cleveland Heights.

The sites purchased are in Kleinman subdivisions and front on Munn road, W. 158th and W. 159th streets and Normandy, Lydian and Doris avenues. The Marquard building operation will improve nearly all the lots available in that section, where there has been other considerable building activity due to the extension of the Lorain avenue car service to Kamm's Corners.

Marquard Co. Today Is Displaying Two Homes

— GREENWOOD AVE HOME —

The Phil Marquard Real Estate & Building Co. is formally opening for first showing today, the first two of a series of twenty "true model" homes being built on Greenwood Avenue, off Rocky River Drive, and Daleview Avenue, in the Lakewood Heights section, just north of Hilliard Road—both locations overlooking the Metropolitan Park system. The houses which will welcome visitors today are at 17113 Greenwood Avenue and 17616 Daleview Avenue.

These homes will be in Spanish, English, French and colonial architecture. The home pictured above is an example. The exterior is of solid brick, certified with the bronze seal of the Clay League, stucco and timber construction, with variegated wood stained shingle roof. In this plan the home is built "around the chimney," thus providing a real deep fireplace for gas or log fire.

Engaged to Marry Carroll Graduate

MISS EVELYN MARQUARD
CHURCHILL PHOTO

Mr. and Mrs. Fred J. Marquard, 3276 Warren Road N. W., announce the engagement of their daughter, Evelyn Sophia, to Mr. Norbert Anthony Schwind, son of Mr. and Mrs. Henry Schwind, Rocky River Cliff. The announcement was first made to 120 guests at a dinner dance and Christmas entertainment at the home of her uncle, Mr. Phil H. Marquard. Miss Marquard is a graduate of Ursuline Academy. Mr. Schwind is a graduate of John Carroll University.

Marquard Co. Is Buildig Three Classes of Mod

GREENWOOD AVENUE HOME

One of the largest house building programs in Greater Cleveland is being carried out by the Phil Marquard Real Estate & Building Co. on Greenwood, Ferndale, Dartmouth and Ernest Avenues N. W., on W. 163th and W. 159th Streets and in Lakewood on Daleview Avenue. The locations are off Rocky River Drive, north of Lorain Avenue.

Three classes of houses are being constructed: Senior models to market at $15,000 to $20,000 which are being built on Greenwood and Daleview; the medium priced models at $9,800 to $12,800 which go on Dartmouth, Ferndale and Ernest Avenues, and the juniors on W. 159th and W. 165th Streets, which are to be marketed under $10,000.

The English type home shown above, at 17115 Greenwood Avenue, is to be kept open today for inspection by the public. It is in the senior model class.

The smaller home shown is one of the junior models.

Officers of the Marquard Co. said yesterday they are finding a greatly increased demand for new homes and at the present rate the company soon would be back on its 1926 production schedule.

ANOTHER M

167

XI. THE DEPRESSION YEARS

The Great Depression commenced with the stock market crash on Black Tuesday October 29, 1929, which triggered a catastrophic world-wide economic slide. In spite of President Roosevelt's best efforts starting in 1933, the depression wouldn't end until 1941, after the U.S. entered World War II.

Cleveland, with its population exceeding 1.2 million, was then the sixth largest city in the country and its economy was at first resilient. The demand for new houses was at an all-time high in the third quarter of 1929. The Marquard brothers fully intended to satisfy that demand by continuing to build quality "Homes Beautiful."

The Rainbow Subdivisions

In 1929 Phil and John embarked on the largest building program in the company's history and it would surpass their previous 1926 construction record. The Rainbow Subdivisions would become one of the largest home building programs in Greater Cleveland history. Phase One, near Triskett Road and West 146th Street consisted of fifty houses. Forty-eight lots sold in the first four weeks. The furnished model opened to the public on October 6, 1929. According to the Plain Dealer, the model at 3428 West 159th Street was the first completely furnished new home offered for sale in Cleveland's history. The homes were conveniently located off of the newly completed Rocky River Drive, overlooking Metropolitan Park.

Little did the Marquard brothers know what the country and indeed the world had in store for them over the next two tumultuous decades.

New Housing Record

The Phil Marquard Real Estate & Building Company set a new housing record in early 1930. According to the Plain Dealer newspaper, the company had developed homes valued at $3,500,000, which equates to almost $50 million in today's dollars. The property alone was valued back then at a minimum of $2 million. In the article, PH was quoted as saying that if all the Marquard houses were lined up they would stretch for 11 miles and that his new homes housed a population of at least 8,600 persons.

In spite of the nation's economic mess, a September 1930 real estate news article proclaimed that plenty of banks and mortgage companies were still ready to lend mortgage money. PH was quoted as saying that he sold more homes for cash—$65,000 worth—in the first eight months of 1930 than he had in the previous two years.

It was also in 1930 when The Marquard Sash & Door Manufacturing Company was incorporated with the principals being PH, Cleo and Phil Jr.

Rainbow Sub Phase Two

It was full speed ahead with Phase Two of the Rainbow developments, which was the Irvington–Munn Subdivision from West 159th to 165th Streets. Marquard had hired the respected architectural firm of Henry Grieme & Son to come up with new home designs. The most popular seemed to be the English Bungalow. The company opened up another fully furnished model home located at 3420 West 159th Street, off of the newly paved Munn Road. It was described as Cleveland's first Swiss Chalet Bungalow, and it included a two–car garage! Of course all interior and exterior woodwork and trim was produced by The Marquard Sash & Door.

A 1932 newspaper article expounded on another first for "Cleveland's Oldest Home Builder," which was a new series of masonry homes at Munn and Normandy, as well as a series of copyrighted brick and tile homes designed by architect H.G. Vetter. These were moderately-priced homes at $7,500–$15,000 in contrast to pricier ones they had built in Cleveland Heights and Lakewood. The economic times required less expensive housing.

In 1933 Marquard teamed up with the Henry Furnace & Foundry Company of Cleveland to introduce what may have been the area's first new home offered with whole-house air conditioning. It was located at 2066 West 93rd Street.

Even little Vin DeCrane got in on the advertising!

Housing Record Is Made by Marquard in 30-Year Period

The Phil Marquard Real Estate & Building Co. is celebrating this week its 30th anniversary, although it is somewhat older than that, since the company, in corporate form, succeeded in 1901 Phil H. and John A. Marquard and their father, who had been building homes for twelve years.

PHIL MARQUARD

In this 30 years the Marquard company has developed homes valued at $3,500,000 on land worth $2,000,000. If all the houses were placed side by side they would stretch for eleven miles, Phil Marquard says. These homes now house a population of 5,600 persons.

The company, in 1926, moved from 507 Canal Road S. W. to its new factory and sales building at West Lorain Avenue.

Builder Completes First of New Series Masonry Homes

Some of the new ideas in 1932 homes are to be shown today at Munn Road and Normandy Avenue N. W., where the Phil Marquard Real Estate & Building Co. will present the first of a special group of copyrighted brick and tile homes now under construction on plans by H. G. Vetter, architect.

The home is typical of those to follow in this builder's program. It presents a complete masonry home, including lot and garage, within the medium price range.

This design has been adapted to its corner location, with covered passage to the garage, and offers an interior of three-bedroom capacity, in which modern conveniences and decorative effects have received special emphasis. Plastered basement, with wood-floored laundry space; vacu-steam heating plant, tiled kitchen and breakfast room, wiring for telephone and radio extensions are additional details which suggest the added quality which builders are including in this year's small home productions. The Clay League has awarded the home its bronze seal of certification.

WILL SHOW NEW MODEL

Marquard Co. to Display Home Furnished Oct. 6.

Phil H. Marquard, president of the Phil H. Marquard Real Estate & Building Co., yesterday announced completion of the new Marquard surprise model home in Rainbow Subdivision, where 46 lots were sold in four weeks.

This is the first model home built by the Marquard Co. since 1924. It was exclusively designed for Marquard and will be artistically furnished by the Fries & Schuele Co.

The home will be opened to the public on Oct. 6.

PHIL MARQUARD
FRANK MOORE—PHTO

Marquard Starts Large List of New Design Homes

This is the first of the new English type bungalow homes designed especially for the Phil Marquard Real Estate & Building Co., by Henry W. Grieme & Son, architects.

It will be one of the types built in the Marquard company's program of houses for the new year, the first unit of which will be 50 houses.

Excavations already have been made for a number of the homes. Rainbow subdivision off Triskett Road at W. 146th Street and Irvington subdivision off of Munn Road at W. 159th, W. 162d and W. 165th Streets have been chosen for the building program, which will be the largest in the Marquard history.

These houses will range in price from $7,000 to $8,400. The design shown provides five rooms and Pullman breakfast room on the first floor, with space for two additional rooms and bath on the second. Many built-in devices will be used.

HALF MILLION GOES INTO NEW HOUSES

Marquard Co. Buys 52 Kleinman Sites for Improvement.

BY JAMES G. MONNETT, JR.

One of the largest developments of moderate priced homes in several years was announced yesterday when the Marquard Real Estate & Building Co. closed negotiations for purchase of the sites from the S. H. Kleinman Realty Co., National City building.

Fifty-two lots in the section bounded by Warren road, Riverside drive, Lorain avenue and Munn road were taken by the Marquard company at around $125,000.

The houses to be constructed will range in building cost from $7,500 to $15,000 each. The total will be more than $500,000. Construction will be started immediately following completion of paving of several streets which now is in progress, Munn road being almost finished. Each house will be of distinct exterior design. The group will include, Dutch and New England colonials, California bungalows and French small chateau type, while all will contain features for which the Marquard organization has been noted.

This is the initial step in building moderate priced homes by the Marquard Co. and is in response to a heavy demand, according to Phil H. Marquard, president. The company has been engaged for a quarter century in building homes of much greater cost in Lakewood and Cleveland Heights.

The sites purchased are in Kleinman subdivisions and front on Munn road, W. 158th and W. 159th streets and Normandy, Lydian and Doris avenues. The Marquard building operation will improve nearly all the lots available in that section, where there has been other considerable building activity due to the extension of the Lorain avenue car service to Kamm's Corners.

Bungalow in New Section Shown Fully Furnished

The Phil Marquard Co. was host to a large number of interested visitors the past week at its second surprise model home, which is the first comletely furnished bungalow ever shown in Cleveland. Its opening was announced in these columns last Sunday. The house is fully furnished by the Reidy Bros. & Flanigan Co. and is open daily from 1 to 9 p. m.

This home is in the Marquard Rainbow No. 2 subdivision and is located at 3428 W. 159th Street, one block east of Rocky River Drive, off Munn Road. It is within walking distance to George Washington and Our Lady of the Angels grade schools, John Marshall High and the new St. Joseph's Academy.

The layout consists of five well arranged rooms with breakfast nook, bath and ice room on first floor; with plenty of sunlight. All rooms are cross-ventilated to insure the greatest comfort; the second floor is planned for adding extra rooms when needed in the future. The fireplace of antique plaster design and all interior and exterior woodwork was manufactured in Marquard's own mill. The interior finish is done in Tiffany glaze with electrical fixtures, and the wall decorations harmonize with the decorating scheme of each room. The lot is seeded and shrubbed, and the paving on this street is in and paid for.

The Family Business

The Marquard enterprises had always been family businesses and as time went by they became even more so. The 1930 city directories reveal that Phil's brother John remained vice president in charge of the building business. Brother Fred ran the the Sash & Door and Joe was head of sales for the real estate company. Son-in-law Al "Dick" DeCrane was a bookkeeper and later became the office manager for the Sash & Door.

Daughter Olivia's husband, Ed Faulhaber started as a clerk at the real estate company and then moved on to sales. According to a November 1932 newspaper article Ed was the Chairman of the Real Estate Board West Side Roundtable. He opened the first Marquard Real Estate branch office at 16011 Detroit Road in Lakewood. This office specialized in rentals, property management, brokerage and home improvement services. PH believed it was time to start having local offices in the communities in which he was operating. I'm not aware that any other branch offices were opened, probably due to the rapidly deteriorating market.

Sad news hit the Marquards in March of 1933 when John's beloved wife of 27 years, Gertrude, died suddenly at age 52. Now John, like Phil, was a widower and neither would ever remarry. John and Gertrude had six children, Roland, Elmer, Lester, John Jr., Jerome and Mary. All of the boys would join the family business. Mary eventually wed another well-known home builder when she became Mrs. Carl Yedlick.

John (above) and Fred (below) at the
front gate of PH's home ca. 1909

SIGNS TOLD SECRET.

John A. Marquard Tried to Deceive His Friends, But They Discovered He Was Married.

In order not to interfere with his business and at the same time surprise his friends, John A. Marquard of the Philip Marquard Building Co., obtained special dispensation for a secret wedding with Miss Gertrude Brickman, the daughter of Mr. and Mrs. Michael Brickman of No. 152 Chatham street, a well known West Side family.

The marriage was solemnized in the chapel of St. Ignatius college by Father Hartman last Monday morning. Both bride and bridegroom returned to their respective homes immediately after the ceremony. Neither said anything to their relatives and friends, planning to surprise them when they moved into their new home at No. 19 Jersey street.

Mr. Marquard's friends and business associates were on the lookout for a secret marriage, as he had previously stated that he would either have a big wedding or be married secretly. The bridegroom's absence from his office last Monday morning aroused suspicions and after some clever detective work the marriage was discovered. Marquard was not congratulated, however, and he was left to think the secret safe.

Late Friday night members of the Bachelors' club and the Young Men's club of St. Mary's parish, of which the bridegroom was a member, decorated his new home with large signs bearing such inscriptions as, "We are Just Married, Gertie and I," and "We Were Married Secretly, Don't Tell Anybody." Many of the signs were from fifteen to twenty feet long and three feet wide.

A guard was maintained at the house all night and throughout the day to prevent the signs from being removed.

At the corner of Lorain and Jersey streets a large sign was suspended across the street bearing the inscription, "This Way to John and Gertrude's House."

The young couple went to their new home yesterday afternoon and were nearly prostrated when they found that their secret had been discovered. The evening was spent in removing the signs and receiving the perpetrators of the joke.

OPENS SECOND OFFICE

Marquard Co. Puts in Charge E. F. Faulhaber.

The Phil Marquard Real Estate & Building Co. has opened a Lakewood office at 16011 Detroit Avenue under the management of Edward F. Faulhaber, chairman of the Lakewood - West Side Round Table division of the Real Estate Board.

It will specialize in Lakewood rentals, brokerage and management and have a department for complete modernizing service.

E. F. FAULHABER

"The company realizes that its office at 14737 Lorain Avenue cannot adequately serve its many clients in the Lakewood area, and as its rental business has considerably increased, it was decided to improve its service by maintaining a separate office in each territory," said President Phil Marquard.

MRS. J. A. MARQUARD DIES

Funeral for Realtor's Wife Will Be at St. Mary's.

Mrs. Gertrude Marquard, 52, wife of John A. Marquard, vice president of the Phil Marquard Real Estate & Building Co., died suddenly yesterday at her residence, 2920 Jay Avenue N. W. She and Mr. Marquard were married 27 years ago at St. Mary's Catholic Church, 3023 Carroll Avenue N. W.

Besides her husband, survivors are a brother, George W. Brickman; a sister, Mrs. Arthur J. Reitz; five sons, Roland, Elmer, Lester, John, jr., and Jerome, and a daughter, Mary Virginia. Funeral services will be at St. Mary's Church. The time had not been set last night.

Grandfather's 1930 Will

I have a copy of PH's Last Will & Testament dated June 2, 1930, obviously written during better financial times. It's twelve pages long on legal-size paper. There are over two dozen separate bequeaths primarily to Catholic churches, schools and charities amounting to several thousand dollars. One thousand dollars was designated for Masses for the repose of his soul and those of other family members with special mention made of his father and mother. A separate amount of $500 was intended for Mass stipends for his late wife Sophia.

Other large bequests were for the Catholic Charities Corporation of Cleveland, The Ursuline Academy in Cleveland, St. Augustine's Convent in Lakewood and the Franciscan Monastery in Hinsdale, Illinois (where Mark was studying) "To be used for the education of deserving students." Donations included Cleveland's Academy of Our Lady of Lourdes for the benefit of orphaned children, and to the Monastery of the Poor Clares on Riverside Drive.

Smaller amounts were to have been sent to an array of Catholic organizations outside of Cleveland, including charities in the states of New York, California, North Carolina, Louisiana, Washington, Missouri, Iowa, Indiana, Oregon and Washington D.C.

I don't believe this pious and generous man needed to set aside any money for Masses for his soul to enter Heaven's gates.

In addition to the charities, Grandfather intended to leave a large sum to his brother Fred who lived in one of the homes on the estate, allowing him to stay there for at least one year after which a reasonable rent was to be paid. This arrangement was intended to be in partial compensation for his invaluable contributions rendered to the business.

Other large amounts were to be paid to his surviving sisters, Alma McAlleenan and Ida Lindenau and their children. These bequests included additional amounts to be paid from time to time for their families' welfare. He also included in this will his brothers John, Joseph and Fred and nephew Jacob Battes.

The remainder of his estate was to go into a trust with ten equal shares for each of his surviving children. He specified that his daughters were to be treated as equals with his sons.

He noted that:

"It is my wish and I urge upon my said children and each of them, that they be honest, industrious, earnest and upright..."

That is one wish that was fulfilled.

The Band Plays On

Everyone was hoping that times would get better soon and business would come back. Grandfather was an optimist. He was heavily invested in land tracts and new homes, but buyers were getting increasingly hard to find. Despite the economic calamity that gripped the nation he continued business as usual, including his generous charitable donations and family lifestyle

The lavish parties and escapades for which the Marquards were well known persevered. The kids were old enough now to be throwing their own soirees. The ballroom dance floor was getting a workout, especially since Prohibition had finally ended in 1933. In a June 1934 society page article, reference was made to a minor accident that occurred at one such party. Marilyn and Marge Foster were identical twins and beautiful local celebrity actresses/entertainers. They were known to switch roles often, as few were able to tell them apart. It seems a Big House party temporarily solved the problem.

The article states that Marge slipped on a beer bottle and injured her ankle. So for quite awhile afterwards Marge was known as "The one with the limp."

My mother recalled when she was dating Dad, how PH would monitor the parties from afar. He would appear from time-to-time off in a corner or hall, with his thumbs in his vest rocking on his heels, while surveying the activities. Although he was mostly a teetotaler, he always wanted to be sure his guests were enjoying themselves, which often included the consumption of alcoholic beverages. As he advised my Dad in a letter: "There's nothing wrong with having a drink or two, just don't overdo it." Mom always found PH somewhat intimidating and she worried that he may not approve of her as a suitable match for his namesake.

Cousin Clare told me that Grandfather loved to throw parties. She said that sometimes out of the blue he would declare: "I think its time for a party!", often to the chagrin of the girls and the staff as they had to get to work on all the preparations. Clare also commented on how PH would attend the party kick-off but usually retire early to his suite. She also told me how uncles Cleo and Fran had these big masquerade heads, probably paper mache, like the ones you see in Thanksgiving Day parades of clowns and other comical characters. If a party was slow in getting started they would leave the room and reappear wearing the big goofy heads which always livened things up!

The lavish Christmas celebrations also continued during the Depression and the Marquard mortgagees, many in arrears, were allowed to remain at their hearths for the holidays and beyond.

Although considered too young to attend these grown-up parties, Clare would peer down through the heat grate in her bedroom floor which was right over the ballroom to view the festivities. Dorie's writings talk about eavesdropping on her uncles' girlfriends comments:

"I think Phil's the best-looking!"
"Cleo's crazy but he sure can dance!"
"Dauby and Vin are nice but they don't like girls."
"They're engaged."
"Dave's nice but he's so shy."
"I'm crazy about Franny but he horses around and forgets me."
"They all just horse around--they don't care if girls are here or not--they'd rather fool around in the kitchen with the family."
"And those kids--my God--they're all over the place--they just walk right in anywhere and nobody says anything to them."

I really tuned in when I heard one girl say, "Listen--you wanna be careful of those kids--they're sacred cows around here."

This puzzled me. At breakfast the next morning I said, "Grandpa---what's a sacred cow?" Even Grandpa was hysterical by the time we got it all sorted out"...Dorie Faulhaber

My Dad told stories of those parties and how his pa portioned out the alcohol, which he kept hidden under lock and key or some thought in secret panels. When the celebrants ran dry one of the boys would seek out their father to petition for another bottle. Usually within a short time Pa would appear with more spirits for the guests. His sons were convinced that he had secret panels where he hid the bottles but their many searches were to no avail.

Clare remembered those secret panels for another reason. Often when one the little "sacred cows" wandered into Grandfather's home office he would plunk them into his big red leather easy chair and say: "I wonder if the boogeyman has anything for you today?" He would then go to a cupboard or closet (or secret panel) and retrieve some candy for the children; always with the solemn admonition: "Now don't tell your Mama!"

Grandfather's home office with his favorite red leather chair (1942)
Vin DeCrane ca. 1930

Footlights and Bright Lights

BY GLENN C. PULLEN.
Comedy of Errors.

Those chanting twin sisters at the Back Stage, Marge and Marilyn Foster, are so uncannily alike in appearance that even their romances are going haywire . . . Stanley Marlowe, who played the pompous army officer in "Pursuit of Happiness," recently, lost his heart to Marge but was embarrassed one night upon finding that he was saying sweet nothings in Marilyn's ears . . . That peeved Johnny O'Moore, one of the Ohio's actors, but he also fell into the amusing comedy of errors by mistaking Marge for Marilyn . . . Both should feel happier after reading this, for there is one sure way of identifying the twins . . . While at Phil Marquard's party at his Warren Road home Marge slipped on a beer bottle and wrenched her knee, so she now walks with a limp . . . But what will the boys do when her limp disappears?

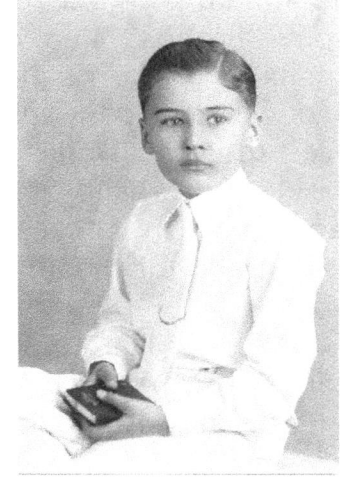

Top: 6/3/34 PD Archives. Above: PH with Rita and niece Connie ca. 1928. Right: Al DeCrane Jr. & Clarice DeCrane 1940

1940

Good Natured Fun

Hard times continued and the cash flow and reserves were drying up. My father related to me how he had many meetings with his pa attempting to get him to reduce spending. Although PH was a practical man in most matters, it didn't seem to apply to his charitable giving or the family traditions. Dad speculated that Pa just couldn't imagine not having the money to live the way he had. So the donations carried on as did the annual July 4th picnic. The annual picnic at the Big House was well attended by family, friends, clergy and neighbors, featuring lots of expensive fireworks. I've heard some of the stories about those wild Independence Day parties. Apparently—at least once—the boys started roman candle wars, shooting bursts of fireballs at each other. The story goes that Francis met his future wife, Sarah Jane McDowell, when he accidentally hit her in the posterior with a roman candle burst!

Vin "Sonny" DeCrane sounded puzzled when I asked him about the fireworks displays, as he recalled fireworks were banned in Cleveland sometime in the late 1930s. However, he did remember a story back when he was just a kid and how one of his uncles created a "firecracker gun" out of some pipes fashioned in an L shape. They would drop a lit firecracker in the barrel and then fire off the make-shift gun. They showed him how to do it and he fired off a few blasts behind the house. Out of nowhere a Cleveland police car roared up and threatened to arrest him for violating the fireworks law. Vin looked for his uncles to explain and save him, but they were nowhere in sight. Shaking in his shoes, fearing imminent arrest, he faced the police alone. At the last minute his uncles reappeared laughing hysterically. They had called a policeman they knew in order to play a prank on their unsuspecting nephew!

Vin's sister Clare also remembered pranks played on her and the other little kids by her uncles. The Marquard property abutted 32 acres owned by Al and Bessie Impett who resided on Rose Lane. One or more of her uncles convinced the kids that if they trespassed onto that land, Mr. Impett would get them and they would never be seen again. Being curious kids, they ventured ever closer to the forbidden property but never saw the dreaded Mr. Impett. After awhile they were convinced that they had been made fools of and that he didn't exist. So they flaunted the rule and crossed on to the Impett land. Out of nowhere the mysterious neighbor appeared! Just the mere sight of him, along with their active imaginations, caused them to flee screaming for their lives! I'm sure that Mr. Impett was a fine person who had no idea why the children ran from him. But the ploy worked and never again did Clare or her playmates consider crossing the property line.

"We six grandchildren had the run of the entire place. Our leader was "Sonny" DeCrane, who was two years older than his sister "Clarie" and I. My twin brothers, Don and Dave, were two years younger than we girls. Sonny and Clarie's brother Al was the twins' age. We were extremely well-behaved children. Our parents didn't put up with much. Consequently, we were welcome almost everywhere. Our favorite rooms were the ballroom, the Chapel and our uncles' bedrooms."...Dorie Faulhaber

Bobby Schwind (cousin), Al DeCrane Jr., Clare, ? and Vin DeCrane on the merry-go-round ca. 1935.

The Marquard Homebuilders, Inc.

In addition to the Phil Marquard Real Estate & Building Company and The Marquard Sash & Door, a third eponymous company also came into being, the Marquard Homebuilders, Inc. I'm not sure when it started up or what the differentiation was to the real estate & building company. Perhaps the intent was to succeed the old Phil Marquard company and to better recognize the contributions of his brothers, John and Joe. Another theory is the new company would handle new home building and the other just the real estate side of the business.

The Filmar Mortgage Co.

I've come across family papers regarding The Filmar Mortgage Company located at 1405 Guarantee Title Building in Cleveland. The company name was a modification of Phil Marquard.

With mortgage money drying up, PH apparently decided to fill that void and grant buyers loans to purchase his homes or to secure second mortgages when the original loans went into default. The company also wrote land contracts for those who were unable to obtain conventional financing. One of the Marquard advertising slogans was "Never a Foreclosure." As times worsened, homeowners were losing their jobs and unable to make their house payments. By the Fall of 1933 almost 50% of American mortgages were in arrears and there were 1,000 foreclosures per day. According to my dad, PH wouldn't foreclose on his debtors and kept granting them more time to pay. I'm sure his Christian values made it very difficult, if not impossible, to put families out on the street.

The New Deal mortgage relief program, the Home Owners Loan Corporation (HOLC), began buying up loans between 1933 and 1935 and extending very favorable terms to those in foreclosure. This federal rescue program made it no longer necessary for Filmar Mortgage and other similar companies to continue operations. As a result Grandfather was able to shut down the firm. However, outstanding loans were still being accounted for at least as late as 1941. The 1940 balance sheet for the Real Estate & Building Company shows a liability for Filmar Mortgage of $94,000. That equates to $1.5 million in 2014 dollars.

Most of the Filmar homeowners never forgot the lifeline that PH extended to them. In later years it produced much goodwill for the Marquard businesses.

The Montrose Co.

About 1933 PH did start taking action to protect his assets and ensure that the companies with his name on the door would continue through the hard times. He desperately wanted his children to inherit the fruits of his labor. After consultations with Carl Schaefer, his longtime attorney and adviser, Grandfather created a family holding corporation and named it the Montrose Company. He served as its president, daughter Verona DeCrane was treasurer and Phil F. served as secretary. Verona, Phil F. and Cleo were directors of the firm. All ten children received shares of stock in the company.

Initially, this holding company may have been designed to hold the vacant lots of the Montrose Street subdivision that evidently remained unsold or not built on due to the Depression.

In December 1933, about a year after son Phil graduated from Georgetown Law School, PH appointed him as his attorney, although he still retained Carl Schaefer from the firm of Schaefer & Schaefer.

In reviewing old records I found reference to an appellate

court judgement against PH in favor of (ironically) a Mr. Loser. Grandfather's attorneys were waiting to see if Mr. Loser would accept the judgement or demand a trial. PH apparently was inclined to file a motion to take the case to the Supreme Court. I have no idea what the proceedings were all about and I found no other references to it. Through 1930 census records I did locate the family of John Loser who owned a home at 532 Rose Lane, near Regnatz's. The record shows Loser was in the restaurant business. I'm guessing he was the individual involved in this matter.

I'm not sure if there's a connection but in 1934 PH appears to have transferred all of his stock in the mill, real estate and building companies to the Montrose Co.

Records indicate that this holding company lasted until the late 1940s.

Chowderheads

In 1936 Vincent, Francis and David signed up for three years in the Ohio National Guard and were sent to Fort Knox Kentucky for training.

"That was a funny thing now the way he and his older brothers, Vin and Fran, had been tricked into the National Guard. Having been riding enthusiasts for some time, they had decided to enter the cavalry, and had gone off without permission of their father, affectionately if not openly termed 'the Guv'nor'. David could still hear Pa's voice crackling with impatience, --"You chowderheads, you young chumps! The three of you joining some fool thing just to ride horses!"

The crowning indignity of all came, when the State cavalry was abandoned and converted into the field artillery three days after the boys joined. So, they were doing all their riding on cannon wagons. Of course, things looked brighter when two cousins and nine best friends joined also, to keep them company. Two of the boys were sons of Cleveland's popular Judge Hurd, the Judge by the way, had a few choice words to say on the subject himself."....Dorie Faulhaber

One of the Hurd boys was Paul who married my mother's sister Virginia Wertz. Virgil Terrell was also in the same Guard unit, he became a physician and was our family doctor for many years.

Fran Marquard at Ft. Knox KY 1936

Top: Vin Marquard. Bottom: Virgil Terrell (?)
with arm around Paul Hurd. Ft. Knox 1936.

The Great Depression Drags On

All of the speculation that the economy would bounce back was not to be. A typical home purchased in 1920 would retain only 56% of its value by 1940. In 1933 the national unemployment rate average hit the record of 25%. However large cities fared much worse. For example Cleveland, Detroit and New York suffered 50% unemployment in 1932. Toledo was at an astounding 80% rate. Times were grim indeed.

During the years 1930–33 President Hoover convened several summits at the White House with businessmen to find solutions. Phil H. Marquard attended some of these meetings. For other meetings he sent his son Phil F. to represent him, since he was in Washington attending Georgetown University Law School. President Roosevelt continued these business roundtables.

My father used to reminisce about meeting several Presidents going back to Calvin Coolidge. He never forgot shaking his hand. He told us "Silent Cal" had a very weak handshake which Dad termed a "fish hand!" He also met Hoover and I think Roosevelt at the roundtable meetings.

Both my grandfather and my father were lifelong Roosevelt Democrats. They always believed that the Democratic party better represented the workingman rather than big business and the rich, which is somewhat ironic considering the family financial status in those years. They never forgot their roots.

While growing up, my father would take us older kids to the Democratic fundraisers. We saw John F. Kennedy and Hubert Humphrey, among others, at the annual Euclid Beach steer roasts. My older brother, Phil, was able to shake Kennedy's hand. We also campaigned for JFK by handing out leaflets and putting up signs and posters.

In 1934, largely as a result of FDR's spending programs, the economy began to come back to life. The administration embarked on what was known as the Second New Deal from 1935 to 1936. By 1937 unemployment had dropped to 14%. The Federal government's spending on public works brought much business back into the Sash & Door and home sales began to show signs of life.

In 1936 the family rejoiced at the marriage of Adelbert "Dauby" to Bertha "Dolly" Wagner.

Back row - Dolly's brother, Phil & Fran Mar... ...Weber, Vin Marquard, Dauby the groom
Front - Jim Wagner, ?, ?, Dolly the bride, Rita Marquard, & Vin De Crane

Bridal Pair in East

MRS. ADELBERT M. MARQUARD
—Marquard

Miss Bertha Rose Wagner, daughter of Mr. and Mrs. John Wagner, 15710 Lydian Avenue S. W., and Mr. Adelbert Michael Marquard, son of Mr. Philip H. Marquard, 3220 Warren Road S. W., were married Feb. 1 in Our Lady of Angels' Church. Miss Catherine Kelley of Bellevue was maid of honor; Miss Rita Marquard, bridesmaid; Doris Jean Faulhaber and Vincent DeCrane, niece and nephew of the bridegroom, were flower girl and ring bearer, and James Wagner, nephew of the bride, was train bearer. Vincent L. Marquard was best man and two other brothers, Messrs. Phil. jr., and Francis Marquard, with John and Leonard Wagner, the bride's brothers, ushered. Frater Philip Marquard, O. F. M. another brother, assisted at the mass. The couple went east for a trip.

Continued Divestiture

The year 1938 brought a resurgence of the Great Depression and further worsened the home building environment. It appears that PH was losing hope that the economy would improve in time to save what was left of his crumbling business empire.

In a 1938 unsigned "Transfer of Gift" document, he gifted to his three daughters all of his jewelry, silverware and the entire household furnishings and belongings located at his home at 3260 Warren. It was understood that everything would remain in place during his lifetime but that ownership belonged to Verona, Olivia and Rita. I'm guessing he was concerned about the possibility of losing these items during a potential bankruptcy or personal lawsuit. I don't know if this document was ever finalized. Between 1938 and 1941, PH gifted all of his certificates of stock in The Marquard Sash & Door to his children equally.

According to the December 31, 1940 balance sheets for the Phil Marquard Real Estate & Building Company and the Marquard Home Builders, the companies owned about $86,000 in vacant land. That equates to almost $1.5 million in 2014 dollars. Taxes had to be paid on the lots but due to the economy there was little sense in building on them.

In 1938 Roosevelt's power was eroding. Conservatives gained seats in the mid-term elections and no new recovery legislation was passed and spending on the New Deal programs was cut in an attempt to balance the budget. The country's unemployment rate jumped to 19%. People saw the previous years as a false start and became, once again, pessimistic and tight-fisted. Not a good formula for selling houses. However there was some good news, Vin wed Mary Jane Brennan on October 12, 1938.

Rev. Philip Marquard O.F.M.

One of the last jubilant events of the decade was my Uncle Mark's ordination into the Franciscan priesthood. He became the Rev. Philip Marquard O.F.M. when he pronounced his solemn vows on June 29, 1939.

Naturally, the Marquard family threw a huge party for him on the eve of the Ordination. Vin DeCrane recalled that his brothers even cleared out all of the vehicles from the attached four-car garage, and the separate but also attached, "Cadillac garage", so named as PH's Cadillac limousine was kept there. The boys cleaned and decorated the garages for the overflow guests and late night partying. It was a hot day so the cool garage areas also provided some relief.

Fr. Philip's legendary career with the Franciscans lasted until his death on April 20, 1986 at the age of 73. Uncle Mark always knew his calling was to work with people for whom the rest of the world did not care about. He was assigned to Chicago in 1940 where he founded the St. Philip Center for the poor and homeless. He went on to help establish St. Anthony's Inn for ex-offenders, St. Joseph and Mary Homeless Shelter in Chicago, Pilgrim Shelter in Harvey, IL, St. Francis Soup Kitchen in Chicago as well as the Chicago Food Depository. He also founded the St. Francis Retirement Village for elderly Catholics, outside of Ft. Worth, Texas, the first of its kind in the U.S.

At one point in his long career he was director of the Alverna Retreat House in Indianapolis where he first began working with ex-offenders. Later he was assigned to Chicago's St. Peter's in the Loop where he became director of The Third Order of St. Francis; now known as the Secular Franciscans. Fr. Philip served as Managing Director of the Franciscan Herald Press and authored many books and articles.

In 1963 Uncle Mark personally presented the St. Francis

Peace Medal to Martin Luther King. He also served with him on President Kennedy's civil rights advisory group. My dad told me that Fr. Philip marched with Dr. King, probably at the violent 1966 Chicago demonstration.

These are just a few of his many accomplishments. It's no surprise with such a grueling work schedule that in 1971 he suffered a massive heart attack. Experimental surgery kept him going for another 15 years.

The Rev. John Egan had this to say about him:

"I have never met a man with more compassion, if St. Francis were alive today his name would have been Philip Marquard."

St. Francis was also from a wealthy family but chose to spend his life among the poor and the outcast.

Fr. Philip also served as the Marquard family priest who officiated at most of his nieces and nephews weddings— and sadly—at relatives and friends' funeral Masses ,including his father's and so many of his brothers.

"When Uncle Mark left town, we all felt a new wave of homesickness.....this 'middle' uncle of the seven Marquard uncles, was the heart and center of the whole family...he wrote each of us a letter on our birthdays, was the most faithful correspondent ever, had the sweetest disposition, the firmest handclasp, the warmest smile, the best advice, the deepest reserves of faith and love - - what did we ever do to deserve him?"....Dorie Faulhaber

I will also never forget getting those wonderful birthday and Christmas letters and religious gifts. We treasured the rosaries blessed by the Pope, some had a crucifix that contained a relic from a Saint. Somehow he always found the time to remember each of his over two dozen nieces and nephews as well as his many other relatives and friends. He was simply an amazing and much–loved and respected person.

I'm quite certain that Marcus* was his father's proudest achievement. His life really deserves its own book. There's an honorary street named for him in Chicago near St. Peter's In the Loop Catholic Church on Madison Street, "Fr. Philip Marquard O.F.M. Way. To further honor his legacy, in 1990 Chicago's Franciscan Outreach services were housed in the newly-named Marquard Center.

*He was always referred to by family as Fr. Philip, Mark or Markie never as Marcus.

Mark (left) was reputed to be an excellent athlete and loved baseball.

Fr. Phil's 1st Mass 7/2/39 Our Lady of Angels-
Al & Vin DeCrane altar boys-Clare DeCrane leads the
procession with Bishop McFadden.

Claire De Crane Walsh

The garage area where the preordination
festivities were held and
Uncle Mark the Novice on far right.

Fr. Philip with Pope Pius XII and Martin Luther King

A Peace Offering: Cited by the New York Organization of Franciscans for his "Franciscan-like approach to the solution of racial problems," the Rev. Martin Luther King Jr. receives the 1963 St. Francis' Peace Medal from the Rev. Philip Marquard.

Franciscan Hits Objections To Award to. Dr. King

NEW YORK (NC) — An official of the Third Order of St. Francis called objections to the group's presenting its 1963 St. Francis Peace Medal to Dr. Martin Luther King a sign of "confusion." Father Philip Marquard, O.F.M., of Chicago, presenting the Peace medal to Dr. King, said the Third Order had encountered objections from "a goodly number of people" to the choice of the Negro integration leader for its honor.

Father Marquard said he thought those who objected were "sincere" and commented:

"But this indicates what confusion exists even in the minds of upright people, and again reflects just one of the many problems Dr. King is faced with in his unselfish task."

Dr. King, a Baptist, is president of the Southern Christian Leadership Conference. In selecting him for its 1963 Peace Medal, the Franciscan Third Order cited his "truly Christian approach to the civil rights problem through his program of nonviolence."

Dr. King, accepting the award, said it signaled "a new level of fellowship and concern" in the civil rights effort. He called it "dear and meaningful" as his first award from a Catholic group, and said he accepted it for his companions "in the front lines of this difficult struggle."

"The crisis of our age," he declared, lies in "the challenge to make the principle of democracy a reality, to make Christian ethics a reality."

Dr. King said a successful outcome of the civil rights effort requires getting rid of certain "myths" — including the idea that, left alone, the problem will solve itself and the idea that "legislation can't solve this problem."

"It may be true that morality can't be legislated," he said, "but behavior can be regulated. It may be true that law can't make a man love me, but it can keep him from lynching me."

The Chicago Catholic   April 25, 1986   24

Fr. Marquard dies at 73

Father Marquard

A Mass of Christian Burial for Father Philip Marquard, OFM, was offered April 23 at St. Peter Church, 110 W. Madison. Father Marquard, 73, who devoted most of his life to helping feed the hungry and provide shelter for the homeless, died Sunday in Chicago Osteopathic Medical Center.

Father Dismas Bonner, minister provincial of the Sacred Heart Province of the Franciscans, was the principal celebrant of the Mass for Father Marquard. Burial was in Mayslake Cemetery, Oak Brook.

Father Marquard, who came to St. Peter Church in 1959, recently founded the Pilgrim Center for the homeless in Harvey. His commitment to help street people in Chicago was also evident in his starting of the St. Joseph and Mary Shelter for the homeless, Harrison Street and California Avenue, and the St. Francis Center, 122 W. Kinzie, a soup kitchen.

HE ALSO helped establish St. Anthony's Inn in Chicago for ex-offenders and the Chicago Food Depository, a surplus of day-old and leftover food that went to the city's hungry.

Ordained in 1939 in Teutopolis, Ohio, Father Marquard moved from his native Cleveland to Chicago one year later. He was assigned to St. Augustine Friary, 5045 S. Laflin, where he was stationed nine years. During that time he was involved with the Back of the Yards Council, organized by Joseph Meegan and Saul Alinsky.

He also founded the old St. Benedict Center for young black people at 28th Street and Dearborn and old St. Philip Center for Mexican youth at 46th Street and McDowell while at St. Augustine.

In 1949, Father Marquard was assigned to Alvernia Retreat House in Indianapolis. He stayed there 10 years, working on a building and expansion program that was designed to help ex-offenders readjust to society. Those who didn't have a place to stay were invited to find refuge at the retreat house.

Father Marquard returned to Chicago in 1959 and was assigned to St. Peter Church, where he worked with the Secular Franciscans (formerly called the Third Order of St. Francis).

OTHER ENDEAVORS Father Marquard has been involved with include founding and directing the St. Francis Village for the elderly in Crowley, Texas. He also helped establish the Mission Volunteer Community at Poverello House on Chicago's West Side and the Queenship of Mary Secular Institute for lay people who have taken their vows.

Father Marquard is survived by three sisters, Verona DeCrane, Olivia Faulhaber and Rita Markle; and, one brother, Vincent.

Wednesday, April 23, 1986

Obituaries

Rev. Philip Marquard; worked with the poor

By Kenan Heise

Rev. Philip Marquard, 73, a Franciscan priest, followed the spirit of St. Francis of Assisi, the founder of his religious order, and worked with the poor and those in need.

He helped establish St. Anthony's Inn in Chicago for ex-offenders; St. Francis Village in Texas for the elderly; St. Joseph and Mary Shelter in Chicago and Pilgrim Shelter in Harvey, both for the homeless; St. Francis Center in Chicago, where free meals are served; and the Chicago Food Depository, to distribute surplus and day-old food to hungry people in the city.

Mass for Father Philip, who resided at St. Augustine Friary, 5045 S. Laflin St., will be said at 10 a.m. Wednesday in St. Peter's Catholic Church, 110 W. Madison St. He died Sunday in Chicago Osteopathic Medical Center.

"One time at dinner recently, he told us how his interest in the homeless, the poor, the destitute and ex-offenders began," Rev. Eugene Michel, a fellow Franciscan, said. "He was inspired while in the seminary by a professor who introduced him to the papal social justice encyclicals, 'Rerum Novarum' and 'Quadragesimo Anno.' He felt after reading them that what Francis would have wanted him to do was to work with people whom the rest of the world did not care about."

Father Philip, a native of Cleveland, was ordained in June, 1939, and came to Chicago a year later. He was assigned to St. Augustine Friary. It was the time when the Back of the Yards Council was organized by Saul Alinsky and Joseph Meegan. Father Philip was involved in the organization's founding and was active in it for the nine years he was stationed at St. Augustine's.

He helped start the St. Philip Center for Mexican youth in the area and worked at the St. Benedict Center, which served young black people at 28th and Dearborn Streets.

In 1949, he was assigned to Alverna Retreat House in Indianapolis. He immediately began a building and expansion program. It was while there that he began his work with ex-offenders. If they did not have a place to reside, he let them stay at the retreat house.

"He helped those whom he could, but he was especially interested in the 'once' or one-time offenders who often needed a place to stay or a job to get back on their feet," Father Eugene said. "At one point, he couldn't find work for the men, so he started a business and hired them to make pillows for people to sit on at sporting events."

He returned to Chicago and St. Peter's Church in the Loop. He was assigned to work with the Third Order of St. Francis [now called the Secular Franciscans.] Through the organization, he founded St. Anthony's Inn on West Jackson Boulevard in 1963

Rev. Philip Marquard

for ex-offenders as a residence or halfway house.

In the early 1960s, he served on an advisory group to President John Kennedy on civil rights with Rev. Martin Luther King Jr.

He became deeply involved with the street people of Chicago and started the St. Joseph and Mary Shelter for the homeless at Harrison Street and California Avenue; the St. Francis Center, a soup kitchen, 122 W. Kinzie St.; and, just recently, the Pilgrim Center in Harvey.

Father Philip began and continued to work with the Chicago Food Depository, which collects day-old or extra foodstuff from supermarkets and delivers it to food pantries and free dispensaries throughout Chicago.

He served for many years as the executive secretary of the Third Order of St. Francis and involved its members in the corporal works of mercy that he helped initiate.

Survivors include three sisters, Verona DeCrane, Olivia Faulhaber and Rita Markle; and a brother, Vincent.

Fr. Phil Marquard, O.F.M.

ARCHIVES

"WHEN I WAS HUNGRY, DID YOU FEED ME? WHEN I WAS HOMELESS, DID YOU GIVE ME SHELTER?"
— FR. PHIL MARQUARD, O.F.M.

Special thanks to everyone that helped in gathering information and photos of Fr. Phil

There are so many great "pillars" in the Franciscans; it is hard to decide on who we could talk about in an article under "Archives". One friar who always comes to mind is Fr. Phil Marquard, O.F.M. Denise Thuston, the Archivist for the Franciscan Province, gladly gathered a great deal of information from her files. Then Fr. Al Merz, O.F.M., a good friend of Fr. Phil, added his 2 cents! Fr. Al decided to ask a few people who knew Fr. Phil for their thoughts. Before long, we received 41 pieces of mail with personal stories about Fr. Phil! His Franciscan love certainly influenced so many people!

Fr. Phil Marquard was the founder of the Franciscan Outreach Association, a haven for the forgotten in Chicago's inner city. He spent his life feeding, clothing and housing the less fortunate.

Fr. Phil distributing food

St. Francis Retirement Village
Crowley, Texas

Fr. Phil was born in Cleveland, Ohio in 1912. He entered the Franciscan Order in 1932 and was ordained a priest in 1939. He cared dearly about the dignity of all people. As a Friar he learned that social justice coupled with compassion for the poor was both a vocation and an opportunity to serve God.

Friars are called to live the Gospel life. Fr. Phil embraced that call to combine prayer and service to the needy. He depended on the generosity of others to sustain his special ministry.

In Fr. Phil's own words, "Our faith and our vocation to our Franciscan Order are not only special privileges, but are also added responsibilities. With prayer and interests in others you can bring them the joy that you have. We must not keep our light under a bushel basket. It must be for all to see. So your life should reflect your inner union with Christ. We are called to serve Christ in others around us. We must speak and act for God to denounce and overcome all forms of injustice and exploitation. We must remember that we truly serve God when we are socially concerned about others."

Marquard Center today

10   THE FRANCISCAN REPORTER • WINTER 2011

XII. THE HEARTBREAKING WAR YEARS

In 1939 the country slowly got back on the road to recovery thanks to the resurrection of the stimulus programs and pre-war spending on the armed forces. But the damage was done and the housing industry would not come back to life until after World War II. Sadly, not all of the family would live to see the recovery.

Hitler's invasion of Czechoslovakia and then Poland in September of 1939 brought war to Europe. Americans knew it was only a matter of time before they would be swept up in the conflagration.

The start of the war coincided with PH's youngest son's graduation from John Carroll University.

"A few words of the last speech caught David's attention, "this approaching war". He would be the first to be drafted, perhaps followed by his brothers, except for Mark who was a priest, there were five others very eligible for conscription.

Seated in another section of the auditorium, David's father sat, tortured by the same thought....There was the immediate probability of losing five or six sons.".....Dorie Faulhaber

As predicted, very early in 1941 David and Cleo were among the first to be drafted into the Army. In March of 1942, at age 33, Philip enlisted in the U.S. Coast Guard. All three of them were unmarried, although David was recently engaged to be married to Virginia Weidt.

"The whole family breathed a sigh of relief when at last, David fell under the spell of a lovely, dark Irish girl, whom he had met casually at a Carroll party. Ginny seemed to fit into the family as did the other boys' young wives, and she never made the mistake of asking him to spend all of his time with her to the exclusion of his brothers.

Thus David stood on the threshold to success, in marriage and the business world...but it was not to be. The summer before Pearl Harbor brought him the expected notice from the War Department.

David read the telegram in a clear voice, as the family lingered over dessert. He got no further than the very official word 'Greetings!' when he was interrupted by a roar of laughter from his brothers. Even Pa was laughing. Good! This was what he wanted, no tears of parting, just the usual raillery."... Dorie Faulhaber

The other boys had draft deferments. Adelbert (Dauby) was 31 years old with very poor eyesight, married to Bertha (Dolly) Wagner with a two-year old son, Marcus. Vincent, age 29, who had served in the Ohio National Guard, was wed to Mary Jane Brennan with one year-old Jimmy. Francis, another National Guard veteran, was age 26 and married to Sarah Jane McDowell. During the war years Uncle Fran worked for Monarch Aluminum, a defense contractor and son Francis Jr. (Jay) was born during the war. In 1939, Mark was ordained Fr. Philip O.F.M. so he was exempt from the military. Dick DeCrane and Verona had three children: Vincent, Clarice and Al Jr. Vincent actually served in the U.S. Army occupation forces at the tail-end of the war. After the war ended he was given a choice to stay in and finish his time or accept an early discharge. Being anxious to get home and complete his college education he chose the early discharge. He laughed when telling me the story because his life was interrupted once again when the Korean Conflict commenced and he was called up to serve since he hadn't completed his full military service.

Jack Sherer and Rita were married with children: Diane,

Marita and Phyllis. Ed Faulhaber and Aunt Olivia (Honey) had Dorie, and the twins, Don and Dave.

After the U.S. entered the war in December, 1941 the majority of the country's resources were focused on developing and manufacturing military material. Peacetime industries like automobiles and home building ground to a halt. The manufacturing sector converted to war footing. That included The Marquard Sash & Door, which discontinued its usual business of fine architectural millwork and began to manufacture wooden ammunition boxes and various other containers for use by the Allied Armies. This production didn't require their workers' usual level of craftsmanship but it kept the company's doors open.

There was a lot of anti–German sentiment in the U.S. as a result of the war. I'm sure that as much as Pa worried about his boys, the three stars on the the front door made him proud as did his habit of flying three American flags over the front door.

The family kitchen table gathering place (1942)

208

Concern Observes 50th Anniversary

Phil H. Marquard is celebrating the fiftieth anniversary of the founding of the Marquard Sash & Door Co., of which he is president He pioneered in the woodworking business along the Cuyahoga River at Canal Road S. W., vacating the site because of the Union Terminal in 1925.

Since 1925 the sash and door company has been operating at 14735-37 Lorain Avenue where also is located Marquard Home Builders which has the same president. A display division has been established by the sash and door company. Eric W. Blackburn, formerly of Beck & Wall Displays, has been retained to head a division designing and developing ideas for conventions and traveling units and displays. •

Top: Philip, PH & Cleo

Left: PD Archives 5/26/40

Bottom: Phil in back of estate and David's U.S. Army portrait (1942).

209

West Park
Sends One of Every 40 to War

Phil Marquard, with three sons in service, is shown here with nine of his 12 grandchildren, left to right: Clarice De Crane, 13; Donald Faulhaber, 11; Alfred De Crane Jr., 11; Phyllis Sherer, 3; David Faulhaber, 11; Marita Sherer, 4; Dianne Sherer, 5; Edwin Faulhaber Jr., 3; Doris Faulhaber, 13.

MISS VIRGINIA WIEDT
Higbee-Chesshir-
left

Mr. and Mrs. R. H. Wiedt, 1516 Lauderdale Avenue, Lakewood announce the engagement of their daughter, Virginia, to Lieut. David J. Marquard, 3260 Warren Road S. W., son of the late Philip H. Marquard. Miss Wiedt attended St. Joseph Academy. Lieut. Marquard, a graduate of John Carroll University, is stationed at Camp Gordon, Ga.

The author's mother Betty Wertz with Ginnie Weidt ca. 1942

PH Sacrifices his Home to Save the Business

By June of 1942 the Marquard enterprises hit bottom causing Grandfather to take desperate measures to assure the future viability of his companies. He made a short-term collateral loan deal with the bank in exchange for sufficient cash to keep the businesses in operation. Evidently, he had six months ending November 15, 1942 to "make good" on the transaction or he would lose his beloved Warren Road home along with all of the other houses and structures on the estate, including their furnishings.

The following are some excerpts from a letter he wrote to my dad who was on active duty with the U.S Coast Guard:

"...this is the better way for the family and the boys and it will give me a chance to come back. I will do all I can to make good. Carl Schaefer and Jake (Battes) thought it was about as good as I could do....I am glad the shop is now taken care of and I would like to have some rest for a short time..."

On September 15, 1942 PH signed a document with the heading, "Instructions to My Children":

"While I have transferred, either directly or indirectly, everything of which I am possessed, nevertheless, I desire to submit the following suggestions for your sincere consideration, after my death."

The document, although signed, appears to have been a draft as it is heavily edited. In it he expressed his desire for monthly Mass stipends as well as other charitable contributions. He named three in particular: Catholic Charities, Parmadale Home for Boys and St. Joseph's Orphanage for Girls. Family documents reveal that the children did their best for many years after his death to follow their pa's instructions.

He also wanted to make certain that what remained of

his estate would be evenly divided between the children, but with special consideration to Adelbert and Vincent for their sacrifices by remaining in the employment of the Mill and their efforts to put it on a profitable basis. He also desired that the children who were still living in his house be charged something to compensate for their living quarters.

"Just as Uncle David starred in my happier early grammar school days, so did Uncle Vin (third youngest) become a special part of my high school days. It was my privilege and pleasure to bum a ride with him over and back - - what HE got out of it I wouldn't know, but Uncle Vin is nothing if not obliging. He has always been eternally cheerful, perpetually busy, clever as an elf, handsome, loyal and a lot of other good stuff.

He was and is the family 'fixer' and resident daredevil. His propensity for climbing up anything high enough to intrigue him makes it easy to pick out his wife in the group below -- she's the one with the out-stretched arms!"...Dorie Faulhaber

Vin Marquard with nephew
Al DeCrane Jr. ca. 1931

In another document PH desired that, if practical, after his death he thought it would be nice if the home could be remodeled into apartments so the children who so desired might reside there with their families. This is a perfect example of how much he loved the house and of his emphasis on the family staying close. It also makes me think that he would have been pleased that the place survived all these years as an apartment house.

MRS. PHILIP MARQUARD, JR.
Trout-Ware

Miss Elizabeth Wertz, daughter of Mr. and Mrs. Austin L. Wertz, 1281 Bunts Road, Lakewood and Mr. Phillip Marquard, jr., son of Mr. Phillip Marquard, 3260 Warren Road, Lakewood, were married Sept. 29 in St. Luke's Church by the Rev. Fr. Phillip of the Franciscan Order, from Chicago. Lieut David Marquard and Mrs. Paul J. Hurd attended the couple. The bride and groom left for Duluth where the latter is stationed with the United States Coast Guard.

Phil & Betty's wedding day 9/29/42

PH raises a toast to the newlyweds. Clockwise: Virginia Wertz the bride's sister, Phil, Betty, Mary Jane, Fr. Phil, Vin, the bride's mother Laura & PH

Grandfather Finally Gets to Rest

My father, Philip Frederick Marquard, was the last of the children to marry. On September 29, 1942, shortly before his 34th birthday, Dad ended his bachelor lifestyle and wed Elizabeth (Betty) Wertz. It was a quiet ceremony at her parish, St. Luke's Catholic Church in Lakewood. As was his father's wish, Pa hosted a breakfast reception after the wedding. Philip was in the Coast Guard and used his leave for the wedding and then made a quick return to Duluth, Minnesota with his new bride. The wedding celebration was the last time he ever saw his beloved father.

About two weeks later, on October 14, 1942 Philip Henry Marquard died at the age of 74 in the house he

214

built and with the family he loved, much the same as both his father and my father did.

Vin DeCrane recalls him being "flat on his back" in his bedroom for several days, with doctors coming and going. Newspaper accounts said that his illness was brief. According to my dad the cause of death was uremic poisoning. Today that condition is known as uremia or chronic kidney failure. There was no good treatment for it in 1940. It wasn't until 1945 that researchers began experimenting with dialysis. I have to think that Grandfather knew for some time that he had the condition. Evidently, he took good care of himself in his later years and his brother-in-law, Dr. Wise, was a physician. There are many symptoms with the disease and they don't just show up in the final days. If he did know then he also would have been aware that the prognosis was grave. This knowledge may well have influenced his family and financial decisions in the last few years. Many of the aforementioned financial maneuvers and final writings and wills seem to give this theory credibility.

The three-day wake was held in the home on Warren and was visited by a throng of clergy, local dignitaries, neighbors, friends and scores of family members. He was laid out in the music room in his full dress Knight of St. Gregory uniform. His granddaughter, Clare, recalled how each of the sons kept a vigil and prayed at the casket all night long for each of the three nights. She said it was a very sad time and having the casket in the home for so long was very spooky for a small girl.

"The death of his father was the worst shock of his twenty-five years. He rode the dirty, antiquated southern train home for the funeral.

He maintained his composure with the family, who sensed it was best to let him work out his loss alone.

At twilight, David went slowly down the hall to his father's rooms and lowered his aching body into the wrinkled red leather chair, that had always been Pa's favorite. His thoughts drifted back two years, to the day he had left for the army. Here in this room, they had shaken hands gravely, each fearful of betraying emotion. Now David wished some of his feelings had not been left unsaid. God knows, he had loved his pa more than anyone. He missed him already so much it was unbearable.

Later that evening, his brothers found him kneeling beside the coffin, his face in his hands, his shoulders shaking with the grief he could no longer suppress.

The seven brothers were united then for the last time on this earth."...Dorie Faulhaber

Phil H. Marquard's funeral Mass was at Our Lady of Angels Catholic Church, of which he was a founding member. There was an honor guard by the Knights of St. Gregory and the Knights of Columbus. The Requiem High Mass was sung by his son Fr. Philip, who was well-known for his wonderful voice. Bishop McFadden along with the Pastor Fr. Linus officiated, with dozens of priests and the sisterhood in attendance. Bishop McFadden expressed his high regard for him and noted "His long life of exemplary Catholic manhood and charity to many causes."

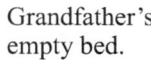
Grandfather's empty bed.

Death Takes Phil Marquard, Builder and Catholic Leader

Phil H. Marquard, a leader in the building field in Cleveland for 46 years and prominent in lay activities of the Cleveland Catholic Diocese, died early today in his home at 3260 Warren road.

Mr. Marquard, whose generosity to Catholic charities was wide in scope, had been ill only a short time.

Fifteen years ago he was made a Knight Commander of the Order of St. Gregory the Great by Pope Pius XI.

Mr. Marquard had built hundreds of homes throughout Greater Cleveland in his long career as a building contractor. He was one of the pioneer developers of the old West Park district and built early homes in Lakewood and East Side developments.

He was founder and president of the Marquard Home Builders Inc. and of the Marquard Sash & Door Manufacturing Co. Associated with him in those concerns were his three brothers, John A., Joseph C. and Fred J., who survive him.

Mr. Marquard was a member of the Builders' Exchange, Lakewood Council Knight of Columbus, a Mason, Cleveland General Assembly, Fourth Degree, Knights of Columbus.

He was the father of 12 children, 10 of whom survive: Mrs. Verdonca DeCrane, Mrs. Olivia Faubhaber, Mrs. Rita Sherer, Corp. Cleo J. at Camp Knox, Ky.; Phil N. Jr., with the U. S. Coast Guard at Superior, Wis.; Adelbert, Father Philip of the Franciscan Order in Chicago; Vincent, Francis and Lieut. Darls J. at Camp Gordon, Ga.

Besides his children and brothers, he is survived by his sisters, Mrs. Louis J. Wise, Mrs. Henry Lindeman and Mrs. William McAleenan, and 13 grandchildren.

A requiem mass will be offered at 10 Saturday morning in Our Lady of Angels Catholic Church, of which he was one of the original members. Friends will be received at the residence.

Mr. Marquard . . . a generous man

Wednesday, October 14, 1942

Phil Marquard, Home Builder, Is Dead at 74

Philip Marquard, 74, president of the Marquard Homebuilders, Inc., and of the Marquard Sash and Door Co., died today in his home, 3260 Warren road, Lakewood, after a brief illness.

Mr. Marquard, who built thousands of Cleveland and Lakewood homes during the 46 years he was in the business, had paralleled in promoting small homes in the real estate developments.

Active in PHILIP H. MARQUARD Catholic church work, he was known for his donations to many of Cleveland's institutions. He always preferred that his bequests remain anonymous.

Once Honored by Pope

Mr. Marquard was a member of the Builders Exchange and a fourth degree Knights of Columbus. In an impressive ceremony in St. John's Cathedral in April, 1928, Mr. Marquard had two other Clevelanders received the insignia of the order of Knight Commander of St. Gregory the Great bestowed upon

---

P. H. Marquard To Be Buried Tomorrow

Dies at 74

Phil H. Marquard, 74, prominent real estate dealer and builder who in 1928 was made a Knight of St. Gregory, will be buried tomorrow following a Requiem Mass at 10 in Our Lady of Angels Church.

Mr. Marquard, the father of 10 living children, died early Wednesday morning at his home after a brief illness. He had been comparatively active in his business affairs until he became ill.

For the past 40 years his name was prominent in the real estate and building business. He was president of Marquard Home Builders, Inc., and also president of the Marquard Sash & Door Manufacturing Co. for that length of time. In both of these companies he was associated with his three brothers, John A., Joseph C. and Fred J. who survive him. Mr. Marquard was a member of the Builders Exchange and a fourth degree Knight of Columbus. He was knighted in the Order of St. Gregory by the late Pope Pius XI.

Besides his brothers, he leaves three daughters and seven sons—Mrs. Verona DeCrane, Mrs. Olivia Faubhaber, Mrs. Rita Sherer, Corporal Cleo J. and Lieutenant David J. of the Army, Phil Jr. in the Coast Guard, Adelbert J., the Rev. Marcus Marquard, O. F. M. of Chicago, Francis and Vincent L. and three sisters, Mrs. Louis J. Wise, Mrs. Henry Lindeman and Mrs. William McAleenan. Two of his children, and his wife, Sophia, preceded him in death.

The Marquard residence at 3260 Warren Road.

Phil H. Marquard

the Ladies Catholic Benevolent Association of St. Joseph's Parish. She leaves a son, Theodore W. Kostrins; a daughter, Mrs. Carrie Wilkinson, and two brothers W. H. and Dan Nugent.

* * *

PHIL H. MARQUARD

Funeral services for Phil H. Marquard, prominent in Catholic and real estate circles, who died Wednesday morning at his home, 3260 Warren Road N. W., were conducted yesterday at Our Lady of the Angels Church, 2644 Rocky River Drive N. W.

The solemn requiem mass was sung by his son, Rev. Philip Marquard of Cr. . . , a priest of the Franciscan order. Rev. Linus Koenigsdorf, pastor of the church, and Rev. Elwin Bloss, assistant were deacon and sub-deacon, the former preaching the sermon.

Also in attendance were Auxiliary Bishop James A. McFadden and a number of priests from parishes throughout the diocese. Several of the sisterhoods were also represented.

Knights of Columbus and Knights of St. John, in both of which Mr. Marquard was a member, formed an escort of honor.

In a brief address Bishop McFadden expressed his high regard for Mr. Marquard's long life of exemplary Catholic manhood and of charity to many causes.

Burial was in St. Mary's Cemetery, W. 41st Street and Clark Avenue S. W.

ARRANGED G. RICHARDS.

Bestowed by Archbishop Joseph Schrembs

The papal honor was bestowed upon Mr. Marquard because of his aid to the needy and his untiring work in the St. Vincent de Paul Society. The honor was bestowed by Pope Pius XI.

Survived by 10 Children

Mr. Marquard was the father of 12 children, 10 of whom are living. Surviving are the children: Mrs. Alfred C. De Crane, Mrs. Edward F. Faubhaber, Corporal Cleo J. Marquard, Philip Marquard Jr. of the Coast Guard, Adelbert M., Rev. Philip Marquard of the Order of Franciscan Monks, Vincent L., Francis J., Lieutenant David J. Marquard, and Mrs. John Sherer; his brothers and sisters, John A., Joseph C., and Fred J. Marquard, Mrs. Louis J. Wise, Mrs. Henry Lindeman and Mrs. William McAleenan, and 13 grandchildren.

Services will be conducted Saturday at 10 a. m. at Our Lady of Angels Catholic Church, 2644 Rocky River Drive. Friends may call at the Marquard home until the hour of the services. The A. B. and C. F. Nunn Funeral Home, 11401 Detroit Avenue, Lakewood, is in charge of arrangements.

218

Top left: PH & Verona at Vermillion cottage. Right: One of his last photos. Below: The last formal portrait of Philip Henry Marquard.

Life on Warren Unravels

Life was difficult enough between the Depression and the war but now with the loss of their beloved patriarch, the family was caught up in a maelstrom. Even as the aftermath swirled around them, they were served papers that all of the property, homes and buildings on the estate now belonged to the bank and everyone residing there was notified to vacate.

Time ran out and Grandfather did not live to "make good" on the earlier referenced bank payment that was due November 15th, thirty days after his death. I'm not certain of the details of the the deal he struck with the bank which provided the capital to keep the businesses afloat. The late Don Faulhaber thought that the arrangement allowed PH and family to stay on the estate until his death at which time the bank would take ownership. PH was one of the few businessmen of the time that would not consider declaring bankruptcy. He insisted on paying his debts and leaving something behind for his family.

So the estate was lost but the businesses remained viable for years to come. The fact remained that everyone on the family compound had a short window to find new lodging. I can't say for sure who all lived on the property in November of 1942. However, in 1940 there were about 62 people living on the estate based on U.S. Census records. According to that 1940 census, living at 3260 Warren, in addition to PH, was Phil Jr., Cleo and David who by 1942 were in the military but still showed the Big House as their residence. They suddenly found themselves without a home address. Al & Verona DeCrane with children Vin, Clarice and Al Jr. lived in the house as did Rita and Jack Sherer with children Marita, Diana and Phyllis. Also included in the census were servants Helen Zelenka, Lucille Franklin, Mary Arcuri and listed as a gardener, John Berkley.

Son Adelbert resided at 3262 Warren with his wife Bertha and son Marcus. Francis and Sarah Jane were listed as living at 3282 Warren. At 3208 were Vincent, Mary Jane and son James. Living at 3276 Warren were brother Fred, Laura and children Constance, Richard and one servant, Anna Kindred. Olivia Faulhaber and family had moved to Cincinnati but had recently returned to a new home in Rocky River.

Anthony Regnatz resided at 3218 Warren along with some restaurant employees. Ted LaBuda and family were at 3206 Warren. There are others listed on various estate properties as lodgers.

The Spanish-style house at 3256, which was built as a wedding present for Verona and Al DeCrane and later lived in by the Faulhabers had been rented out to Edwin Brauer and family.

The 1940 census shows all of these folks living on the estate as renters, except of course the family scion,
Phil H. Marquard.

The bank gave all of them 30 days to vacate the premises and make new arrangements.

"Grandpa Marquard died. THE BIG HOUSE had to be sold. The earth trembled.

I couldn't bear it. I thought it over and decided that Grandpa would so hate anyone living there but us, that I would be perfectly justified in setting it afire.

So I rode my bike from my Rocky River home, 2-1/2 miles away, back to Grandpa's with two packs of matches and a can of lighter fluid in my pocket. You guessed it. Why is it you can never get a good fire going when you plan it but the merest spark can create a disaster other times? I ended the afternoon flat on my stomach under my favorite tree -- sobbing." ...Dorie Faulhaber

The Estate Sale

On Sunday November 15, 1942 this notice appeared in the Cleveland Plain Dealer newspaper:

Private Sale

3260 Warren rd.,

Lakewood, Ohio.

Sun., Nov. 15th,
Mon., Nov. 16th

Entire household furnishings
of the late Phil Marquard

Also have children's outdoor play
yard equipment.

Sale starts at 10 a. m. through to !
p. m. Conducted by Joseph H. Zwee

According to the after-sale inventory there was a total of around seven hundred items sold during the two days. The sale brought in about $6,000, or $90,000 in 2014 money. Everything from the grand piano ($250) and the grandfather clock ($125), clothing, the monogrammed Royal Doulton china etc., went out the door. PH's sons and daughters purchased many items that were special to them including many of the paintings on tapestry ($100–$250 each). Vin DeCrane recalled that the grandfather clock in the foyer was so big that as a little tyke he could climb inside and hide behind the pendulum.

In our household we grew up with three of those paintings, some oriental rugs, a few tables and my grandfather's bedroom set. I still use his mahogany dresser. We also had a set of monogrammed tableware that included a teapot and creamer which I retain. I never knew that my dad had to purchase these items.

Almost all of the religious paintings, statues etc. were

donated by the family to The Poor Clares and to Our Lady of Angels Parish as well as other local churches. The largest donation was the family's Blessed Virgin shrine that stands today in front of the Poor Clares' Convent on Rocky River Drive in Cleveland.

The final inventory and settlement of the Grandfather's estate was completed in December of 1942. After expenses, debts and distributions to the businesses, it appears his children received a little over one thousand dollars each. The settlement included not only the estate sale receipts but all of what was left of their father's cash, savings accounts, life insurance, etc. My dad told me how people assumed they all inherited a great fortune and were set for life. When he was job hunting, one prospective employer even questioned why he wanted a job as he was sure Dad was worth a fortune. If they only knew.

The Family Home is Sold

The Marquard home of 35 years was sold by the bank for an undisclosed price to William Bauer who was described as a packing company president. He in turn leased it to the U.S. Government for conversion into a fifteen-suite apartment house for war workers' families. Bauer also purchased the adjoining "wedding present house" at 3276 Warren. The conversion work was handled by the Federal Home Owners Loan Corporation. Paul J. Ockert was contracted as the remodeling architect and Dunlap & Johnston general contractors of Cleveland Heights performed the work.

An interesting side note, it turns out that sometime later cousin Vin DeCrane was hired by John Dunlap to do yard work at his home. He was so impressed by Vin's work ethic that after Vin received his architectural engineering degree from Notre Dame, Dunlap hired him into his firm.

Years later Vin became co-owner and president of Dunlop & Johnston Inc, General Contractors.

According to the newspaper account the plans called for there to be two suites of two rooms, ten with three rooms, six with four rooms and one each with of five and six rooms. A total of 69 rooms between the two houses, which probably did not count bathrooms or basement rooms. The mansion already had six complete suites built for family members so the conversion was made somewhat easier. The third and fourth floor of the mansion were not used due to fire ordinances. A recent check of the Zillow website shows the building today as having 18 apartments and 18 bathrooms, 12,702 square feet situated on close to an acre of land.

I'm sure Grandfather looked down from Heaven with tears in his eyes as he watched the unraveling of his once splendid home and fortune. But, I think he would have had some solace in knowing that his sacrifices enabled the businesses to stay in the family and that needy and deserving folks would reside under his big roof for many years to come.

Marquard House to Make 15 Suites

Amazing Home of Late Builder Leased to U. S.

By JAMES K. CHANDLER
Real Estate Editor

The amazing 52-room home of the late Emil B. Marquard, builder and business man, today was leased by the Government from its present owner, William Bauer, packing company president, and will be converted into a 15-suite apartment house for war workers' families.

Screened from the street by heavy shrubs at 3260 Warren road, the huge home stands in an arbor of big trees. An adjoining home at 3276 Warren road, also built by Mr. Marquard and purchased by Mr. Bauer, has been leased to the Government for conversion into four suites.

Back in 1912, Mr. Marquard purchased a moderate-sized farmhouse on the grounds and this farmhouse became the nucleus of the high, wide and interesting Marquard home.

As Mr. Marquard's family grew, more rooms and wings and floors were added to the farmhouse until it finally reached the 52-room total. There were 13 children.

Has Complete Chapel

In the home is a complete chapel, which was blessed by Archbishop Joseph Schrembs.

On the roof is a "sky apartment" which was built for one of Mr. Marquard's sons, who was in ill health. A sun room the size of a ballroom is on the ground floor of the north wing. Three garages are built into the rear of the home.

From the front, with its towering pillars and curved portico, the appearance is of Georgian architecture. From the rear, with several sets of outdoor stairways, gables and chimneys, the appearance is of Bavarian architecture.

Mr. Marquard had a suite of rooms for himself in the rear of the home. Other suites were used by the children, some of whom lived there for a time with their own families, after they were married.

Since the Marquard home already has five suites with kitchens and baths, extensive alterations will not be required. The third and fourth floors will not be used, in accordance with fire protection ordinances.

Three Heating Plants

There are three heating plants in the basement, two of them being auxiliaries to a large boiler which takes a ton of coal a day to fire, when the whole house is in use.

When work is completed in both houses, there will be two suites of two rooms, 10 with three rooms, six with four rooms and one each of five and six rooms.

When the home is converted into

Front view of the former Marquard home.

Rear view shows many additions, "sky apartment."

apartments, these will be rented to war workers through the War Housing Service in Public Square, Mrs. Katherine Patch, WHS manager, said today. The conversion work is being handled by the Home Owners Loan Corp. The Government will pay Mr. Bauer a small "net profit" rental, assuming all taxes, upkeep and other charges on the property, as well as costs of conversion.

"There is a great need for more homes and buildings to be converted to apartments," Mrs. Patch said today. "Any realtor can give property owners full information or they can get it here at the WHS office."

Cleveland Press 6/21/43

Brothers in Arms

The family all got resettled in their new homes and life went on despite their losses. However life was far from normal due to the raging war and the fact that so many family and friends were in the midst of it.

"I kept busy mailing packages and writing letters to three of my Marquard uncles, Cleo, Phil and Dave. I very much resented the fact that they had to go 'off to war' whether they wanted to or not."... Dorie Faulhaber

By 1944 Cleo, who was in the 91st Evacuation Hospital Army Medical Corps, arrived in England after a long bloody tour of duty in North Africa and Sicily. There he was to await word on the forthcoming D–Day invasion. In March or April of 1943 Cleo had a tumor removed from under his arm that left him unable to use that limb from the elbow down. He underwent physical therapy to recover the usage. It's possible that his ailment may be how he ended up in the medical corps but I can't say with any certainty.

Phil, still in Coast Guard Port Security, was stationed in Duluth, Minnesota with wife Betty. On May 8, 1944 she gave birth to Philip Frederick Jr. (Another Philip to contend with!) David, who was in London, was honored to be Phil Junior's Godfather.

Fr. Philip, Betty & Phil Jr. enjoy some leave time

"Shortly after being promoted to first-lieutenant, he received a call to the office of the commander, David had been chosen to lead a special field group of men to do intelligence scouting work for the coming invasion. He was given a pre-Christmas leave as a reward for signing away his life.

Arriving home one week before Christmas, he was caught up in a whirlpool of eager relatives, each determined to do something for him before he left for the invasion.

Christmas morning was spent at the home of his younger married sister, Rita. After breakfast he wandered into the living room and stood for a long moment before the picture of his father. The youngsters soon began opening their gifts, running to Uncle Dave with each new acquisition. He thoroughly enjoyed watching their antics - if only this lump in his throat would melt. Suddenly he jumped to his feet, muttered hasty goodbyes, and plunged blindly down the front steps to his waiting car.

His small nephew inquired anxiously, "Why was Uncle Davy crying, Mom?"

At midnight, Christmas night, all the family gathered at the train station. Standing there, a tall trim figure in khaki (records show him being 6'2" 165 lbs.), he laughed and talked carelessly slapping his yellow pigskin gloves against his leg in an old familiar gesture.

Tension mounted as the moments passed; no one dared put his feelings into words. At last Dave, after making formal goodbyes, raised his hand in a casual salute, and said shakily, 'Well this is it; so long folks'"....Dorie Faulhaber

Sadly, this scene was somewhat typical all across America and Europe for so many families.

Thousands upon thousands of Allied soldiers poured into the London environs preparing for the largest invasion in world history. What are the odds that one evening in early May, while relaxing in a London pub that David would hear a familiar voice in the crowd. It just so happened that his eldest brother Cleo showed up in the same pub! There was quite a reunion and for the next few weeks the brothers were inseparable. Dave also located his cousin, John Marquard Jr. that first week of May and they spent a good part of the day together catching up and reminiscing. John was an Army Technical Staff Sergeant. Dave spent much of his free time hunting up friends and relatives; all in the same place for the same reason, to win the war and return home.

A letter David wrote, dated May 21, 1944, may have been the last that the family received, it closed with these prophetic words:

"I appreciate the prayers and novenas you have had said for me. Please keep them up. I need them.
Best of luck to all......Dave."

By D–Day, June 6, 1944, the band of brothers once again parted; each off to do their duty in the horrific war. The next time Cleo heard news of Dave was on June 19th, when one of his patients in the field hospital told him that he had spoken to David the day before and that he was safe, after a difficult battle for which his company was to receive a citation.

Cleo sent a V-Mail letter home dated on the fateful day of June 22nd:

"I often think of Dave, it certainly must be hell where he is at present. I have not received any news about his battalion since I talked to the patient from his unit. I hope you are having a lot of Masses said for us at this time. An Army chaplain has been saying Mass in an old French church here on the edge of this area. I have been going every evening at 6:30 PM. It is a real treat to kneel on a church bench again." (7)

Cleo was working twelve hour shifts from 8pm to 8am in the field or the hospital.

When Cleo wrote this letter David was far from hell; for he had been reunited in Heaven that morning with his father, mother, brother and sister.

They are Corp. Cleo J. Marquard and Lt. David Marquard and Pfc. John Fazekas and Seaman 1-c David P. Fazekas.

Brothers, Cousins United In England, New Guinea

The brothers hadn't seen each other since they were recalled from their respective camps to attend the funeral of their father in October, 1942.

Corporal Marquard, 26, left for overseas duty two months later and spent several months in Africa and Sicily as a member of the 91st Evacuation Hospital Division. A few weeks ago he was moved to an English base and found he was only three hours distance away from his brother David.

"It was the happiest day of my life when I saw David," he writes. "After a year of not seeing the family you can imagine what a wonderful feeling it was."

Lt. Marquard   Corp. Marquard

This clipping from a family scrapbook has a typo showing Cleo's age as 26, he was 37, Dave was 26.

Capt. Leonard T. Schraeder Jr. & David 11/19/42

Our Family Hero

In the early morning hours of June 22nd near Cherbourg, France 1st Lt. David J. Marquard climbed out of his foxhole to receive Holy Communion and face another day of hard fighting. Most of his intelligence squad went out on a scouting patrol while Dave remained behind to guard the battalion command post. He discovered a German patrol had been hiding in a ditch near the crossroads awaiting this moment to attack and destroy the command post. David volunteered to intercept them. The following is from the official U.S. Army citation:

"Lt. Marquard, after hearing rifle shots fired at the guards, immediately went to their aid without hesitation and with disregard for his own danger, although he was only armed with a carbine. He held off the enemy force, pinning them down with his fire until a sufficient force could be brought to bear against them. The enemy patrol was knocked out, but during the fight, Lt. Marquard was killed by enemy machine gun fire. His outstanding courage prevented the enemy patrol from firing on the command post, thereby saving the lives of key staff personnel and preventing disorganization within the unit."

David, who was born during World War I, supposedly "The war to end all wars," died at the age of 26 and was posthumously awarded the Silver Star for Gallantry, the Purple Heart and promoted to Captain. As I previously wrote how my Uncle Mark deserves his own book, the same applies to my uncles, David and Cleo.

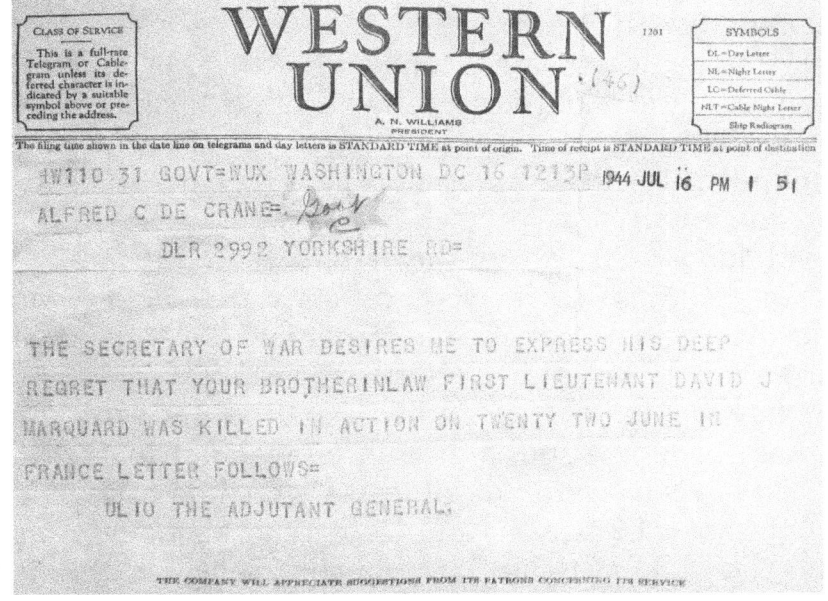

S, TUESDAY, JULY 18, 1944

Lieut. Marquard . . . killed in Normandy.

"Swamped with Grief"

Nearly a month later, July 16th, the official Western Union telegram was received by Verona's husband, Alfred C. DeCrane, notifying the family of David's death. Thankfully, David's Pa was not alive to have to read the grim contents.

Not long after, all of the letters that the family had written to Uncle Dave were returned to sender with a handwritten note on each envelope: "Deceased R.C. Fellows, Capt. 8th Inf."

As fate would have it, Cleo was not that far away on the morning of June 22nd; although he was not located until July 2nd when a trio of officers, who knew Dave well, brought the news to his pup tent. The Major was crying while Dave's best friend, Lt. Johnson, delivered the news. Cleo was prevented from sending the terrible news home until the official telegram had been sent and received. In a letter dated July 27 he recounted his reaction when he was told the news: "I just stood dumbstruck and could only say 'Oh'." The following are more excerpts from that letter:

"On the fourth of July I located Dave's grave. Standing at my pup tent and looking over four hedge rows I can see the crosses of the cemetery from here. I often make a visit to his grave as it's only a five minute walk across the two fields to the cemetery. Standing at the foot of of his grave with one of his dog tags nailed to the white cross, it's difficult to realize that Dave is lying there. One conciliation is that the war is over for him and he is not going thru the hell at the front.

The other day while at the cemetery the French people from the Catholic Church nearby were planting flowers on each grave.

Have Vin take fifty dollars from my account for Masses for Dave.

I feel much lonelier here now with Dave gone. He was our favorite brother and everyone that knew him loved him. No doubt I shall miss him more when I get back to Cleveland. Tell Ginny I am very sorry.

Wishing you and family my love. Please write often.

Yours,

Cleo"

Many cards and letters of condolence were sent to the family. The following are some excerpts.

Major George L. Mabry served with David and wrote to Verona on August 8, 1944.

"No one could have asked for a more perfect gentleman, worker and soldier...David and I looked death in the eyes but never once did I see him falter or hesitate to perform his mission in an excellent manner...I have seen many of my comrades fall in battle but when David was called from us it left a telling scar in my heart...a true friend and a real soldier."

Lt. Colonel Carlton McNeely wrote to Francis on June 9, 1945:

"From the first day day we set foot on French soil, and he crossed the beach with me, it would be impossible to to place into words the great work that he performed...David was beloved by all the officers and men, and all had the greatest respect for his ability and knowledge. He was not only an understanding officer, but one of the finest gentlemen...We had been fighting very hard all during the 20 and 21 June against the outer defenses of Cherbourg. After driving the Germans, we had halted for the night. Early the morning 22 June, David came to my slit trench, and told me that a German patrol was coming down the road to our rear. He asked to take a patrol of men to destroy or capture the enemy...Moving to intercept the enemy, David's patrol was fired upon by a German machine gun, and from that burst of fire David and one of his men were killed...and he died as he lived, with his face toward the enemy."

Cousin Dorie expressed the family's feelings best:

"Dave had always worn "the coat of many colors" in the Marquard family. However, unlike the favored son Joseph in the Old Testament story, no jealousy arose, for it was an honor freely accorded to him not only by his father but by the whole family...and he never knew he had it.

It was hard to believe we would never see him again...never see him blush...never enjoy his wit, never again take advantage of his perpetual willingness to do favors for everyone...after all these years I still want him back...I am a very sore loser.

Our whole family was swamped with grief. I was very worried about Mother who was pregnant with my youngest brother, Alan. I thought she would lose the baby immediately. But she didn't, of course. As for me, tears rolled down my cheeks incessantly any time or any place.

I wrote letters to Dave anyway in childish defiance of those letters returned to me by the Army with that dreadful red stamp on them that said "deceased".

First there was a Memorial Mass - beautiful but unbearable. Then a quick three years later all wounds were freshly opened and salted when his body was returned for burial here. The French cemetery was being closed. This put the kibosh on the dreams of a few of us (I know I wasn't the only one) who were hoping for a movie miracle -- you know -- Dave would be found suffering from amnesia in a Veterans Hospital, he'd be spotted in a London pub where he was hiding out because of a terrible scar, or he'd be located in a German prisoner of war camp where he had been concealing his identity and his secret mission. But we didn't "find" him and he hadn't come back.

Dave's pretty fiancé and I had been very close; now I felt I would lose her too. And I was right. Her family very wisely, eased her out of our clan. She found someone else."....Dorie Faulhaber

12—THE CATHOLIC UNIVERSE BULLETIN—June 8, 1945

Silver Star to Marquard,
2 Padres Rate Bronze

Awards to Cleveland Diocese soldiers for heroism and achievement were announced this week by the posthumous award of the Silver Star Medal to a lieutenant for gallantry in Normandy, and the award of Bronze Star Medals to two priests of the diocese now serving as Army chaplains. One of the chaplains received the award in the form of an Oak Leaf Cluster, having received the same decoration before.

Other decorations were two Bronze Star Medals and the Distinguished Flying Cross.

The Silver Star Medal went to:

FIRST LT. DAVID J. MARQUARD, brother of Mrs. Alfred De Crane, 2692 Yorkshire Road (posthumous).

Bronze Star Medals were awarded to:

LT. COL. JOHN T. MURPHY, chaplain, son of Mrs. Sara Murphy, 4152 E. 99th Street.

CAPT. FRANCIS T. DIETZ, S. J., chaplain, son of Mr. F. X. Dietz, 3271 Tullamore Road, Cleveland Heights.

M.-SGT. VINCENT M. SCHNEIDER, son of Mr. and Mrs. L. J. Schneider, R.D. 1, Avon.

PFC EDWARD T. BORAWSKI, 24, son of Mrs. Rose Borawski, 315 Twelfth Street, Lorain.

The Distinguished Flying Cross went to:

FIRST LT. RICHARD O. WEBER, 21, son of Mr. and Mrs. Frank J. Weber, 13524 Lydian Avenue.

FIRST LT. DAVID J. MARQUARD, killed June 22, 1944, in France, was awarded the Silver Star Medal for the action which resulted in his death.

The citation accompanying the award reads:

"An enemy patrol of two officers and nine enlisted men had been hiding in a ditch near a crossroad, awaiting a favorable and strategic moment to force their way past the guards and deliver fire against Lieutenant Marquard's command post.

"Lieutenant Marquard, after hearing rifle shots fired at the guards, immediately went to their aid without hesitation and with disregard for his own danger, although he was armed only with a carbine. He held off the enemy force, pinning them down with his fire until a sufficient force could be brought to bear against them. The enemy patrol was knocked out but during the fight, Lieutenant Marquard was killed by enemy machine gun fire. His outstanding courage prevented the enemy patrol from firing on the command post, thereby saving the lives of key staff personnel and preventing disorganization within the units."

The lieutenant, son of the late Mr. and Mrs. Phil H. Marquard, was a graduate of John Carroll University. He had been in the Army 2½ years.

Two of his brothers are in service, Corporal Cleo, 30, now in a rest camp near Berlin. He is with a Medical Corps outfit. Shortly after Lieutenant David's death, Corporal Cleo killed; his brother's grave in France. He has 91 points for discharge but expects to be sent to the United States for duty as he is classed as an essential technician. Coast Guard Petty Officer Philip is stationed in Duluth, Minn. Another brother is the Rev. Philip formerly Marcus Marquard, O. F. M., of Chicago.

First Lt. David J. Marquard

For Us They Died That We May Know Peace

peace, for which throughout the ages, millions of lives have been given, today in a weary, war-spent world appears to find no haven. But over those hallowed areas throughout the world where rest the bodies of war's victims, the gentle spirit of peace hovers always and the white crosses which mark the graves of victors and vanquished stand in mute appeal that none of these dead shall have died in vain.

ABOVE: United States Military Cemetery No. 1 at Ste. Mere Eglise in Normandy, France, the scene of bitter fighting two years ago when Americans pushed inland from invasion beaches.

LEFT: Germans who were killed in the Normandy invasion fighting are buried in this cemetery, set up by United States forces at Orglandes, on the Cotentin Peninsula, northwest of Ste. Mere Eglise. These plots are exactly like the American cemeteries, except that there are no names on the grave markers. Those that are known, however, are re-

Uncle Cleo

Despite the loss of their parents, the oldest and youngest brothers and the family home, eventually life went on for the Marquards. Cleo, Phil Jr. and cousin John Jr. all returned home safely at the end of the war. Uncle David was the only family casualty. Although the term "casualty of war" can manifest itself in different ways. Many of "The Greatest Generation" were never quite the same thereafter.

Cleo's hospital team followed the bloody battles, moving on to Holland. Later they were one of the first medical teams to enter Germany and witness the aftermath of the Nazi atrocities. In the years that followed the war Cleo always seemed happy and jovial but inwardly he was a changed man. My dad remarked to me once that Cleo's wartime experiences were horrendous. Although he tried at times to talk to him about it, Cleo was unable to describe his experience without breaking down. The subject was never again raised. He lived life alone—never marrying—in a small Marquard–built 1950 ranch home on a couple of rural acres at 5500 Columbia Road in North Olmsted, Ohio. For companions he had his horse and two Dalmatian dogs. He remained near to family and worked at the Mill. Uncle Cleo was closest to his brother Mark (Fr. Philip) and spent as much time as possible by his side. He would pick him up in Chicago or Texas and drive him back and forth to Cleveland for holidays and family events. Cleo always had a new Pontiac and often drove straight through from Texas. When we would ask how he was able to do that he'd say he would sleep part of the way and let one of the dogs drive! He never lost his Marquard sense of humor. After Cleo retired from the family business he went to work for Fr. Philip managing the St. Francis Retirement Village in Texas. He passed away there in 1976 at the age of 69.

Web photo of the 91st Evacuation Hospital Army Medical Corps. 4th from left top sure looks like Cleo.

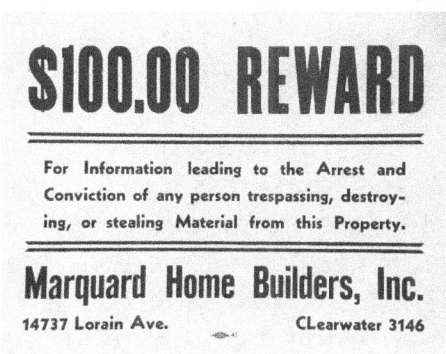

XIII. THE RECOVERY

The war was over and the family businesses survived thanks to Grandfather's foresight and planning. Much credit also goes to his brothers, John, Joe and Fred, his children and other trusted advisors. The building industry was on the fast-track for recovery in large part due to the millions of returning soldiers who were picking up where they left off: job hunting, getting married and raising families. Those families needed homes but they were in short supply. Businesses got off of wartime production and were retooling for the civilian demand.

The Marquards continued to operate for the mutual benefit of one and all. Sadly, right at the peak of the recovery, death was once again visited upon the family.

Fred and Joe Reunited with Phil

Fortunately Grandfather had built a sound infrastructure and leadership team for the enterprise. However the team's first string was getting decimated. In 1944, two years after Phil's death his baby brother, Fred, passed away at age 60. In 1947 Joe died at age 69. Longevity was not a strong suit in this family. The beloved brothers were integral to the business. Joe was head of sales for the building company and Fred was the backbone of The Marquard Sash & Door.

It was now time for the boys to assume more responsibility in the business and they were well-equipped thanks to their training and education. Verona's husband, Dick DeCrane, had worked for the Sash & Door since at least 1930; he now stepped up as president. He also served as vice president of the building company. Vin and Cleo Marquard became vice presidents at the Mill. Adelbert (Dauby) was the mill's secretary–treasurer and general manager.

PH's brother John was now president and chief architect for the building company. His sons Roland, John Jr., Lester, Elmer and Jerome also went to work for the company.

Fred had six children, Evelyn, Joseph M., Adele, Fred Jr., Richard J., and Constance. Richard worked for the building company. Fred Jr. owned a successful painting & decorating company which performed a great deal of work for the family firms.

When my father, Phil Jr, returned from the war he chose to continue his law career. In his early years he had served the family businesses in many capacities. Prior to the war he was employed by the Internal Revenue Service and later worked as an Assistant Special Counsel for the Ohio State Attorney General. After the war he was a Special Agent for the War Assets Administration.

Francis was employed as Vice President of Sales with his father-in-law's company, Ruud Mfg.

Wilfred B. Marquard

Wilfred B. Marquard (1899–1985), had worked as a salesman for the building company since 1928 He was elevated to secretary–treasurer. Wilfred was the son of Bernard A. Marquard who owned a very successful photography studio in Cleveland. Bernard was the son of Bernhard who was an uncle to PH. There was also another family connection. The following is from Wilfred's son Robert's 1996 letter to me:

"I don't know if you know this but to make things more complicated your grandfather's brother Joseph was my mother's (Dorothy Costello) stepfather. Thus I grew up with two Grandpa Marquards and two Grandma Marquards. Actually my dad met my mother at one of the Marquard family parties on Warren Road."

Since Wilfred was too old to serve in World War II he was able to fill the void at The Marquard Building Company (the former Marquard Homebuilders Inc.) and kept the business going during those tragic years. He was well qualified, having apprenticed under his father–in–law, Joseph C. Marquard, for almost twenty years.

Back row: Ed Faulhaber, John murphy, Carl Neff, Wil Marquard groom, Cleo Marquard, Roland Marquard, Bob Mc Carthy, Phil Marquard Jr.
Standing: Honey, Dorothy the bride, Isabel Noble, Mildred Mc Carthy
Seated: Ceil Feighan, Evelyn Marquard.
Flower girl is Letty Marquard

Housing Crisis

The minimal homebuilding during the Depression and World War II, together with the return of millions of veterans, created the worst housing shortage in the country's history. One of FDR's last pieces of legislation was the G.I. Bill. It became law in 1945 and among other benefits provided for low interest home loans with no down payment. Veterans were able to purchase over two million homes thanks to this legislation that was passed unanimously by Congress.

The federal government estimated that another three million houses needed to be built between 1946 and 1947. The demand for most of these homes was among low and middle income families. Many looked to prefabrication as a solution, believing that manufacturing and technical advances generated by the war would result in homes rolling off production lines by the millions.

The prefab trend hurt the Marquard businesses since their stock-in-trade had always been quality construction and millwork. It took awhile but the Mill attempted to adapt by offering prefabricated partition walls, though primarily for the commercial market.

By 1947, 37,000 prefabricated houses were built representing only 6% of all new single-home construction. The reasons for these low numbers were varied. For many prospective buyers, prefabricated housing still carried the taint of being quick and shoddy like the prefabs built as emergency housing during the war. Thin-plywood walls were not a big selling point. Building codes and labor unions were also barriers to that industry.

The Continued Push West

By 1946 the Marquard enterprises were humming along and developing large tracts of land in the the Village of Fairview, a burgeoning western suburb. Marquard "Homes

Beautiful" were popping up one after another on streets in the north central section of town: Belvidere, Stanford, Woodstock, Elmore, and West 204, to name some. These new affordable—mostly three-bedroom colonials—drew hundreds from Cleveland and by 1950 the village exceeded 9,000 residents and was incorporated as the city of Fairview Park.

From 1947 to 1974 our family resided in one of those "Homes Beautiful" at 20533 Belvidere Avenue. It was around 1947 that my father's job at the the War Assets Administration was winding down and he decided to plunge back into the family business. Part of his decision may have been brought about by the realization that none of PH's sons were involved in the building company; most were working at the Mill. Philip Frederick became Secretary for both the Sash & Door and The Marquard Building Company. He worked full-time alongside Wilfred in the building business. Around 1949 they moved the Marquard Building Company offices to 20600 Lorain Road in Fairview Park.

THE

MARQUARD

BUILDING COMPANY

Cleveland's Oldest Home Builders

20600 LORAIN AVENUE • CLEVELAND 26, OHIO

PHIL. MARQUARD, Sec'y   OR 1-3146

Below: Recent photo of the home we grew up in on Belvidere Ave.

XIV. THE FIFTIES

Elvis and Chuck Berry weren't the only ones rocking and rolling in the fifties, "Cleveland's Oldest Home Builder" was in for its fair share.

John August Marquard Passes Away

On April 24, 1950 Grandfather's younger brother John passed away at the age of 75. He was the last of the four brothers who were the scions of the family enterprise. All of them died between 1942 and 1950. Once again Fr. Philip officiated at yet another family funeral. John was a tremendous loss to the building company as he was the Master Builder and chief architect who apprenticed under his father Philip (the 1st) back in the 1890s. He had five sons, one daughter and fifteen grandchildren. John's wife Gertrude (Brickman) had passed away in 1938.

JOHN A. MARQUARD

John A. Marquard, president of the Marquard Building Co., the city's oldest home construction organization, will be buried in St. Mary's Cemetery after services at 10 a. m. Thursday in St. Angela's Catholic Church, Fairview Park.

A nephew, Rev. Philip Marquard. O. F. M., of Indianapolis, will be celebrant.

Mr. Marquard died yesterday in St. John's Hospital at the age of 75. He was the last of four brothers, Philip, Joseph, Frederick and himself all of whom had been associated with the building business founded by their father, Philip Marquard, over a century ago. All the brothers have died within eight years.

The company was believed to have built more homes in the Cleveland district than any other single organization. It also did a large volume of commercial construction. Mr. Marquard's connection with the building industry covered 60 years.

His wife, Mrs. Gertrude Brickman Marquard, died in 1938. Surviving him are five sons, Roland G., Elmer J., Lester A., John P. and Jerome J.; a daughter, Mrs. Carl Yedlick, and 15 grandchildren.

Friends may call at the Charles F. Nunn funeral home, 12629 Detroit Avenue, Lakewood.

John Marquard Sons, Inc.

On June 28, 1950, two months after John Sr.'s death, John Jr. registered a new company: John Marquard Sons, Inc. Officers included Roland, Elmer, Jerome and Lester. The enterprise had its headquarters at 3788 Rocky River Drive in Cleveland. Later the offices relocated to 21665 Center Ridge Road in Westlake.

I can only speculate as to why John's heirs decided to leave The Marquard Building Company and strike out on their own. It may have been a matter of creative differences. Roland, like his father was an architect, and the new company was specializing in larger custom-built homes. During the Forties and Fifties The Marquard Building Company was erecting smaller mostly three-bedroom colonials and ranches for the middle-class buyer. One can drive down the streets in north central Fairview Park and easily recognize these homes. Many of our neighbors and friends all lived in houses pretty much the same as ours. As I recall, John Sr. and sons Jerome and John Jr. lived in those "Homes Beautiful" on Stanford and Elmore in our old neighborhood.

On April 3, 1954 The Cleveland Press newspaper ran a story on my father as part of the "Meet the Home Building Association Trustees" series. The headline was "His Smallest House is Best," referring to the cabin my dad had built in our backyard. We kids enjoyed it as a clubhouse and for summer sleep-outs. My older brother Philip IV, who was age seven at the time, recalls asking Dad what the headline meant. He responded that "Small homes are better because they keep the family close."

John's sons were catering more to the upper middle class with their custom colonial architecture. I first noticed the difference in styles when they developed the Linden Road subdivision just north of Belvidere Avenue. The homes were larger, more stylish and expensive than the ones my dad's company had built in Fairview. The Marquard Building Company retained the rights to the advertising mottos "Homes Beautiful" and "Cleveland's Oldest Home Builder." However, since both firms had their roots in Philip the 1st's 19th century company, John Marquard Sons could also market that heritage, especially since their father was the Master Builder. Recognizing the potential, John's sons continued the push west and began developing Rocky River, Westlake, Bay Village and Avon Lake.

In addition to the creative conflicts, I believe there were also differences concerning financial and investment strategies. It is my understanding that Wilfred, who was treasurer of the old company, was very conservative with the purse strings, believing another depression was just around the corner. There were recessions in 1945 and about every three to four years through 1958 as the country and the Federal Reserve were adjusting to the post-war economy, including the period after the Korean War. Due to these ups and downs it was understandable to be concerned over another possible depression.

There was tremendous opportunity in the western suburbs which had hundreds of acres of former farmland. My father often expressed his frustration at missed opportunities for the company to purchase and develop these lands. He was certain that in the not-so-distant future the value and prices would skyrocket, which of course they did.

Lastly, there's always the ever-present family dynamic that may well have played a role in the breakup. To my knowledge Phil, John, Fred and Joe's families were close and I am not aware of any family feuds, but just the sheer size of the clan along with Wilfred's family would cause me to think there had to be at least some friction. Grandfather was a larger-than-life figure whose name had been on everything. Maybe John's sons thought the time had come to make their own mark and get the well-deserved recognition and rewards.

BIG JOKE their father's telling is the only thing that can keep four lively Marquard children together and still long enough for a picture in their home at 20533 Belvidere Ave., Fairview Park. Huddling around Philip Marquard, a Home Builders Assn. trustee, are Nancy, 2; his wife, Betty; Tim, 4; Philip III, 9, and Tom, 7.

Meet the Trustees

His Smallest House Is Best

The smallest house Home Builders Assn. trustee Philip Marquard ever built is without doubt his most successful.

That house is a one-room plan with real bunk beds in the Marquard back yard at 20533 Belvidere Ave., Fairview Park. To the four Marquard children, Philip III, 9; Tom, 7; Tim, 4, and Nancy, 2, it's a fort, a cave, a ship's cabin and best of all, a place to camp out on hot summer nights.

"Phil and Tom sleep out almost every warm night with their Dad," Mrs. Marquard said. "This summer Tim will be old enough to try, but we're not sure how he'll brave the strange noises."

An outdoors-loving family, the Marquards also spend much of the summer swimming in Lake Erie, and Marquard still keeps in practice on the tennis serve he developed when his family had their own tennis courts at their home on Warren Rd.

Grass Hopeless

The boys are more interested in baseball and have converted the side yard into the neighborhood baseball diamond.

"I put new grass seed in there every spring," Marquard said, looking at the bare "base lines" hopelessly, "but it's really a waste of money. The whole neighborhood seems to be playing here most of the time."

Marquard, who grew up with the building business and is now secretary of the company his father found-

ed, took a busman's holiday not too long ago to build an addition on his own home.

He knocked out the kitchen window, made the hole into a door and built on a roomy breakfast room and combination bedroom-den paneled in mahogany panelette.

"We just couldn't squeeze the whole family into three bedrooms and an average-size kitchen anymore," he explained.

In addition to being secretary of the Marquard Building Co., Marquard, 45, is also secretary of another family business, the Marquard Sash & Door Co., a practicing attorney with a law degree from Georgetown University and secretary of the recently-announced Parade of Homes project in Rocky River.

The Sash & Door Struggles Along

The Mill continued to supply both of the Marquard building companies and many other firms with architectural millwork. However, the days of custom quality craftsmanship were winding down. The push was on for cheaper mass-produced goods and the world economy was gearing up, most notably in Japan. The markets were now starting to offer assembly–line plastics, prefab wood composites and other synthetics at a fraction of the price. A lot of the competition eventually gave up and went out of business. With improved transportation modes and better highways, the Sash & Door was having to compete more often with out-of-state and Canadian companies. The southern states were especially competitive owing to a cheaper labor market. The Mill was unionized back in the 1930s and like most northern companies skilled trade wages were much higher than in the South.

However the firm managed to keep its doors open by downsizing and diversifying. They partnered in the mid-fifties with Wood Products Co. and in 1954 even sold boats on their lot to bring in more income. The Marquard boys were striving honestly and doing their best.

More Family Loss and Big House Resold

In 1955 PH's fourth son, Adelbert "Dauby" Marquard died at the untimely age of 45. He was the first of the brothers to pass away since David's tragic end in 1944. The family once again went into mourning. He was loved by all, especially by his wife Dolly and three sons, Marcus, Bert and Ken.

Grandfather's sister Mary Katie, better known as Mayme, who married Dr. Wise, died in 1956 at the age of 86. Sophia's brother Henry, known as Harry, also died in 1956 at age 78. His widow, Ida Mary (PH's sister), followed a year later at age 82. Of Philip and Mary's twelve children only Alma Lizzie remained. She lived to the age of 92, joining her siblings in 1973.

In 1958 the Marquard Mansion was sold by Jerome Bollotin for $75,000. Bollotin owned Times Square Drug Company. The buyer was Louis Cardinal & Son, who made the purchase as an investment. The newspaper article on the sale stated the house had two 5-room suites, four 4-room suites and eleven 3-room suites. That's 17 suites for a total of 59 rooms.

In 1961 Louis Cardinal resold the house for a nice profit. He received $94,000 ($741K in 2015 $) from East-West Realty who also bought it for investment purposes. A Mr. Laderman owned the property during the 70s and 80s but I'm unsure when his ownership began or ended.

The old behemoth endured as apartments and at some point was named the Manor House. A 1961 photo shows that much of the ornate trim on the facade had been removed. However, it looks like the third floor as well as the rooftop Sky Apartment remained intact, although evidently unused due to multi-dwelling fire codes.

Adelbert's wedding photo 1936.
Obits, Harry 12/14/56 & Ida
Lindenau 9/7/57 (PD Archives)

Henry E. Lindenau, 78, Shoe Sales Figure, Dead

Henry E. Lindenau, who died yesterday at 78, was widely known on the West Side both as a life-long resident of that area and as a veteran of 50 years in the shoe business. His residence was at 3611 W. 148th Street.

Mr. Lindenau began his shoe-selling career as a boy on W. 25th Street. During most of his half century in that business he was manager of stores for the Miller-United Shoe Co. on the West Side and, for a brief period, in Akron.

He was married 56 years ago in St. Mary's Catholic Church to the former Ida Marquard with whom he celebrated their anniversary Nov. 5.

Mr. Lindenau is survived by his wife; three sons, Harry W., Russell and Raymond; a daughter, Loretta, and two grandchildren.

He was a member of the Fraternal Order of Eagles all his adult life and was long active in St. Mel's Parish.

Friends will be received at Corrigan's funeral home, Lorain Avenue at W. 148th Street after 5 p.m. tomorrow.

A funeral mass will be at 10 a.m. Monday in St. Mel's Catholic Church, 14436 Triskett Road N.W. Burial will be in Holy Cross Cemetery.

Mrs. Ida Lindenau

Mrs. Ida Lindenau, member of a pioneer West Side construction family, died yesterday in her home at 3611 W. 148th Street. She was 81.

Mrs. Lindenau was born on Bailey Avenue and was the daughter of Philip Marquard, a builder of many West Side homes. Her husband, Henry, died in 1946.

She was a member of St. Mel's Altar and Rosary Society.

Mrs. Lindenau is survived by three sons, Harry, Russell and Raymond; a daughter, Miss Loretta Lindenau, and two grandchildren.

Time and place of services will be announced later by the Corrigan funeral home, 14750 Lorain Avenue.

Old Marquard Home Sold for $75,000

Landscape contractor Louis Cardinal has purchased a 17-suite apartment house at 3260 Warren Rd. for $75,000.

The brick-and-frame building—former 52-room home of the late Phil H. Marquard, builder—was sold by Jerome Bollotin, who operates Times Square Drug Co.

Cardinal, head of Louis Cardinal & Son, bought the property for investment. Sale was negotiated by One-O-Five Clifton Co.

Located on a 127x200-foot wooded lot, the two-story building has 11 three-room suites, 4 four-room suites and 2 five-room suites.

In 1912, when Marquard bought the property, the building was a moderate-sized farmhouse. As Marquard's family grew—there were 12 children—he added rooms and wings to the farmhouse until it finally reached 52 rooms.

A subsequent owner, William Bauer, leased the home to the Government in 1943 for conversion into an apartment house for war workers' families.

FORMER MARQUARD HOME at 3260 Warren Rd. was sold by Jerome Bollotin for $75,000. Purchaser of the 17-suite building is Louis Cardinal, landscape contractor.

PRICE WAS $94,000 for this 52-room mansion which was converted into an 18-suite apartment. The building, at 3260 Warren Rd., LAKEWOOD, was purchased by the East-West Realty Co. from Louis and Linda Cardinal. The 18-suite building was the former home of the late Phil Marquard, builder.

Lakewood Mansion Sold for $94,000

The former 52-room home of the late builder, Phil Marquard, was sold for a reported $94,000. The large mansion at 3260 Warren Rd., LAKEWOOD, was converted some years ago into an 18-suite apartment building with a monthly revenue of about $1500. Buyer was the East-West Realty Co. who is holding the property for investment purposes. Sellers were Louis and Linda Cardinal. The Cardinals bought the mansion in 1958 for a reported $75,000. Lot size is 160x250 ft. The sale was handled by J. I. Berkenfield of Joseph Laronge Inc.

XV. CLOSING THE DOORS

In the late Fifties, The Marquard Building Company constructed its last subdivision located on Santa Clara Drive in Westlake. But it was one of its best; the colonial homes were larger with more style and features than most that they had built in Fairview Park. They more closely resembled the homes that John Marquard Sons had built in the Linden Road subdivision. Santa Clara featured paneled family rooms, two and half baths, fireplaces, mud rooms and built-in kitchen appliances, including dishwashers. I recall accompanying Dad on Sundays when he had open houses there and was very proud of the well-built quality homes.

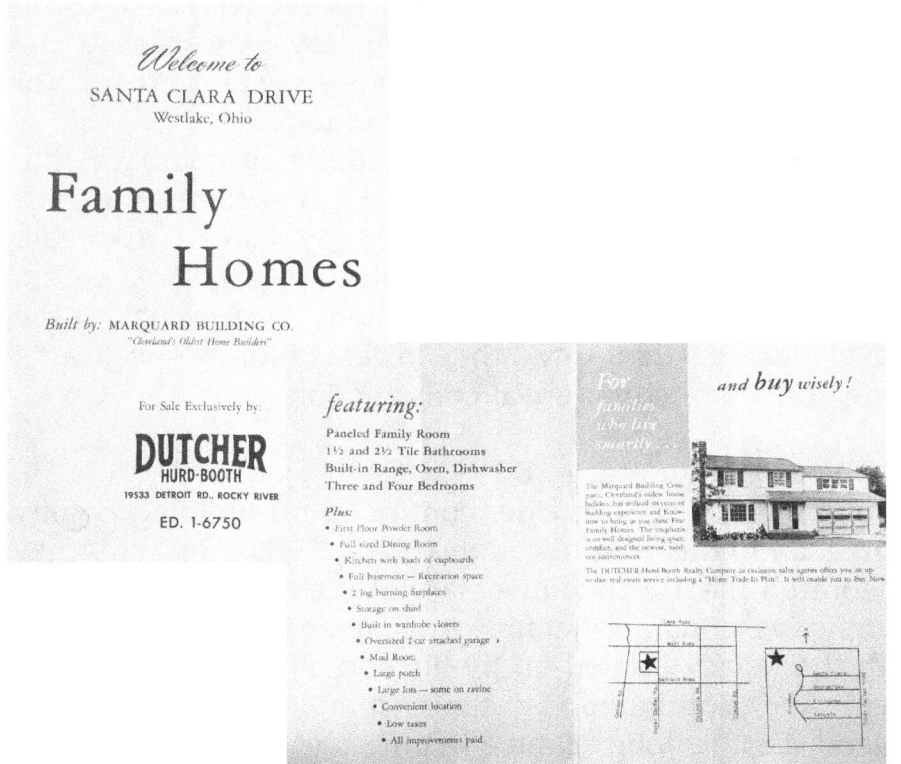

The Marquard Building Co. Shuts Down

The Santa Clara Drive development was the last hurrah for the building company. Between another recession and continued management conflicts, my father decided it was time to move on.

I'll always remember waiting for him to drive up to the house after work in his white 1956 Chrysler Windsor. We kids would run out to welcome him home with the first question being: "Did you sell any houses?" Since so much of his income was based on sales we knew that if he'd had a good day we would all be happy and maybe get something new or go out for dinner. But all too often he would reply with his usual sunny optimism:

"Not today but maybe tomorrow!"

After he sold out his interest to Wilfred Marquard, he worked for awhile as an agent for Dutcher–Hurd–Booth Realty and then returned to his true love, the law. At the end he served as a Cuyahoga County Assistant Prosecutor and part time Rocky River Municipal Judge.

It wasn't long after Dad left the building company that Wilfred liquidated "Cleveland's Oldest Home Builder." Grandfather had started the company almost 50 years earlier, but its roots were with his father's firm, dating back to 1869. The company had built more homes in the Cleveland area than any other organization, as well as a large volume of commercial construction.

100 Year Anniversary 1869–1969

John Marquard Sons, Inc. continued on building quality homes and flourished throughout the 1960s. In 1969 they celebrated the 100th anniversary of the Marquard building companies, which originated with Great Grandfather Philip with the legacy carried on by his sons: Phil, John, Joe and Fred; and continued by their combined sons: Philip, Roland, Lester, John, Elmer, Jerome and Fred. It truly was

"Cleveland's Oldest Home Builder" of "Homes Beautiful!"

Sadly, my father, Philip Jr., was not there to enjoy the celebration, having passed away at his Fairview Park home in November of 1968.

PROFILE IN REALTY

Marquard Has Team, Tradition

Key to the success of the five home-building Marquard brothers is that they work together as a team. They meet as a board to discuss plans. Around one table they represent 150 years of experience.

That is the proud picture of the firm, launched about a century ago, presented by the spokesman for the modern team — John P. Marquard, treasurer and administrative executive.

Others in John Marquard Sons, Inc., 21665 C e n t e r Ridge Road, Rocky River, are b r o t h e r s Roland G. (president), Elmer J. (vice president), Jerome J. (vice president), and Lester A. (secretary).

Imprint of M a r q u a r d craftsmanship can be found all over the West Side, where they specialize. It was started about 100 years ago by Philip M a r q u a r d, grandfather of the present group, who decided Cleveland was an up-and-coming town and a good place in which to build.

HE DIDN'T KNOW it, but he was starting a tradition. It was carried on by his four sons—John (father of the present five building Marquards), Philip, Joseph and Fred. They were in business nearly 60 years, building up much of the lower West Side and extending into Lakewood.

In L a k e w o o d they developed a reputation for unusual millwork, adding special detail in the wood they put into their homes. The streets they helped develop included Chase Avenue, Lake Avenue, Edgewater Drive,

John P. Marquard

Lauderdale A v e n u e, and others.

"WE CAN SHOW original contracts of homes sold by our family in 1910 for the then magnificent sum of $3,400," said John Marquard. "These homes are now selling at $17,000, over four times the original cost."

"We grew up in the business," John added. "We were brought up knowing what an 8-penny nail and two-by-four was because that is all we heard around home."

Even the lone sister, Mary Virginia Yedlick, married a Cleveland builder.

AND THERE IS a good probability the tradition will continue. John, for example, has eight children, six girls and two boys. The oldest, a 15-year-old boy, builds play

houses in the basement and sells them.

Another of the new generation already moving into the field is the son of Lester. Robert is a carpenter journeyman on the job at age 22.

"We are not doing things in the old way," John Marquard hastened to make clear. "We got great training from the older generation, but we are bringing it up to date with the latest techniques. We blend the solid foundation of the past with the opportunities of the future."

HE .NOTED .THAT .the brothers offered "a complete package—right from original planning and architectural service (Roland is a graduate architect), we can design a home in tune with planned furniture."

The company likes to make custom homes. The same architect plans a home whether it sells for $15,000 or for $80,000, they said.

One of their developments was Carriage Circle, on the border between Rocky River and Fairview, where the average home was $60,000. Another was Plimouth Bay Colony with homes at $29,800.

"In putting in modern methods and the latest techniques, we insist that an executive member of the company have direct supervision in every home," Marquard said.

—Marc Gleisser.

HOUSE OF THE WEEK

Split-Level Has an Or

An unusual double roof effect imparts a subtle Oriental

The Marquard Sash & Door Closes 1890-1973

After graduating from Fairview High School in 1965 I went to work for the Mill. I had long harbored dreams of one day returning the company to its former glory. I was hired in at the bottom as a trainee fireman in the boiler room, general laborer and master floor sweeper. I also helped unload and stack the raw lumber from the box cars. I think I still have a splinter or two in my hands as mementos. I worked alongside my Uncle Vin's sons, Jerry and Denny Marquard. They had worked there on and off for several years. I had visions that someday we would be the new generation of Marquards to run the family business. I was young and naive but earning two dollars an hour!

My dad, the company secretary and Uncle Vin who was president, counseled me many times on how the old place didn't have much of a future in the rapidly changing industry. I was often cautioned not to get my hopes up. They were correct of course, which I came to learn after about four months of employment. The company was still using the old belt powered saws and machinery, much of which had to date back to the early part of the century, as did many of the loyal craftsmen that were employed there.

The workers turned out a quality product but profits in this industry were now comprised of volume, high output and cheap labor, none of which the old mill could claim. The family simply didn't have the capital needed to modernize and refit the place to meet the demands of the plywood era. Many of the workers were German immigrants who had been with the company their entire careers and were headed for a well-deserved retirement, as were my uncles Vin and Cleo who managed the old factory. Verona's husband, "Dick" DeCrane, who had been president for many years was already retired; however to my knowledge, PH's surviving children retained their shares in the firm. Working there was a great experience which I will never forget but it was time for me to move on as well. To this day, whenever I catch the the scent of fresh-cut wood, I'm transported back to that glorious place.

In 1973 the Sash & Door closed up and the building and land was advertised for lease. **(8)**

Vin Marquard the last
President of the Sash & Door

PUBLIC SALE

OF WOODWORKING COMPANY

Open Mon., Jan. 15 through Sat.
Jan. 20, 9 a.m. to 4 p.m.

Plywood sheets and cutoff, planed
hard and soft wood cutoffs, mould-
ing, cherry walnut, ash, mahogany, pine, oak, etc.

Formica sheet cutoff, clamps,
machinery, nails, screws, an-
tiques, hundreds of other items.

The Marquard Sash

& Door Mfg. Co.

14735 Lorain Ave.

W. 150th AND I-71

SALE OR LEASE

40,000 sq. ft. 1st floor, 7,000' 2nd, 3
acres. High ceilings, Sprinklered, bed
level dock, Drive-in doors, Rail siding,
Exhaust and air system. Ample parking and room for expansion.

MARQUARD SASH & DOOR CO.

14735 Lorain Ave.   941-5960

Mary Ann Brennan

No history of the Marquard businesses would be complete without giving Mary Ann proper recognition. She was a wonderful lady who went to work for PH as a secretary and bookkeeper way back in 1926. She served as his Gal Friday for all of his enterprises. After his death she persevered, working for both the Mill as well as the building company. She was the go-to person throughout the companies' history. I guess you could say she was like family. (9)

Ms. Brennan was still working at the Mill in 1965 during my employment there. After work she would usually drop me off at the corner of Lorain and West 204th Street. As I recall she drove a 1959 green Chrysler Saratoga with enormous tail fins. What a boat of a car that was!

She was a lovely old spinster by that time but sharp as a tack with a terrific sense of humor. She spent over forty years as a loyal and devoted Marquard employee, friend and valued advisor.

End of an Era

Within a year of my father's death, his brother Francis joined the heavenly family in 1969. He was followed by Cleo in 1976 and both Vincent and Marcus (Fr. Phil) in 1986. My aunts fared better, with Verona passing at age 87 in 1990, Olivia shortly before turning 96 in 2001 and the youngest, Rita, died in 2003. Aunt Rita and family moved to Texas and then out to California back in the early 1950s. Regrettably, I never had a chance to get to know them.

John's sons carried on the building tradition. They developed beautiful west suburban neighborhoods such as Carriage Circle in Rocky River and Plimouth Bay Colony. Around 1980 John Marquard Sons closed but Jerome and I think Lester continued building and remodeling on a smaller scale. Roland died in 1986, Both Jerome and brother Elmer passed in 1988. John Jr. died at age 87 in 2002, leaving behind eight children and his beautiful wife Helen, who lived until the year 2014.

I believe Fred Jr.'s (1914–1999) painting and decorating business, headquartered in Fairview Park, also closed up in the early 1980s. He and his brother Richard were partners originally, until Richard branched off on his own at some point. Much of their work came from the Marquard building companies.

The last known group photo of the remaining Marquard brothers: Phil, Vin, Cleo, Fr. Philip and Francis. Ca. 1967

Philip Marquard Dies, County Legal Aide

Philip F. Marquard, 59, assistant county prosecutor and former judicial candidate and Democratic candidate for mayor of Fairview Park, collapsed and died at home yesterday.

He had returned to work recently after being hospitalized for a heart condition.

Mr. Marquard was in charge of preparing cases to be presented to the County Grand Jury. He was a graduate of John Carroll University and Georgetown University Law School and had studied business administration at Harvard.

He was a former deputy collector for Internal Revenue and an assistant Ohio attorney general. He also served as a law and intelligence officer in the Coast Guard during World War II.

Mr. Marquard was secretary and co-owner of the Marquard Sash and Door Manufacturing Co., founded by his father, and was a former trustee of the Home Builders Assn.

HE WAS A MEMBER of the Cleveland and Cuyahoga Bar Assns., the Fairview Park Democratic Club and St. Angela Church. At his death, he was Democratic precinct committeeman. He had run for mayor of Fairview Park and for Common Pleas and Rocky River judgships.

Mr. Marquard is survived by his wife, Betty; five children, Phillip Jr., Thomas, Timothy, Nancy and Gary; four brothers, three sisters, and a grandson. He lived at 20533 Belvidere Ave., Fairview Park.

Funeral Mass will be said at 10:30 a. m. Wednesday in St. Angela Church. Friends may call at Corrigan's Fairview Park Funeral Home from 2 to 5 and 7 to 9 p. m.

Vincent L. Marquard, owned door business

Services for Vincent L. Marquard, 72, president of the old Marquard Sash & Door Manufacturing Co., will be at St. James Catholic Church, 17514 Detroit Ave., Lakewood, at 9 a.m. tomorrow.

Marquard

Mr. Marquard died Wednesday at St. Augustine Manor. He contracted a respiratory infection after arterial surgery about four months ago.

He started working in the family business as a boy, and did everything from sweeping up to driving a truck on his way up. The business was started by his grandfather in 1890 and its custom millwork can be seen in many large public and private buildings around Cleveland.

Many of the wooden church steeples are Marquard millwork. Mr. Marquard retired in 1972 when the business closed, and after that

spent a lot of time gardening, a longtime interest of his. He built a rooftop garden with planting boxes on top of the garage at his Lakewood home. There, he grew flowers and vegetables, many of which he gave away.

He was a member of the Builders Exchange. He was an usher at St. James Parish and a former member of the parish council. He had been a scoutmaster and merit badge counselor for the Boy Scouts of America. He belonged to the Third Order of St. Francis and the Holy Name Society.

He was the ninth of 12 children and grew up in the huge old Marquard house on Warren Rd. After the children grew up, the house was divided into about 20 apartments. Mr. Marquard attended John Carroll University after graduating from St. Ignatius High School in 1931.

Surviving are his wife, Mary Jane; sons, James, Jerry, Dennis and Vincent Jr.; daughters, Sister Mary Beth and Ann; nine grandchildren; and three sisters.

XVI. Legacy

Phil H. Marquard's legacy stretches far and wide. His good works, monetary and material donations to Catholic churches and organizations in Cleveland and across the United States are part of that legacy. One favorite reminder is the shrine to the Blessed Mother, which stood for years on the grounds of his home and today may be seen in front of the Poor Clare's convent on Rocky River Drive. His generosity wasn't limited to the Church. He gave freely to many worthy causes, often anonymously. I'm sure there are more than a few Clevelanders that still remember how he helped them through the Great Depression, whether by extending their mortgages or providing them with jobs.

Phil and Sophia's children carried on that family tradition; perhaps best embodied by Fr. Philip's Franciscan outreach to the poor, the homeless, convicts and elderly. Uncle David will never be forgotten for sacrificing his life for our country nor will the other sons and daughters who were part of the war effort, especially Uncle Cleo.

In addition to the family's individual and collective achievements, there are also material reminders in the form of the thousands of Marquard-built homes and the distinctive architectural millwork that can be found, not only in homes, but in and on churches and commercial buildings throughout Greater Cleveland.

The Grandchildren

Being devout Catholics, many of the children of Phil and Sophia had between five and eight children, for a total of 29. Verona and Dick DeCrane had three offspring but they produced 18 great grandchildren! By my reckoning, those 29 grandchildren of Phil and Sophia produced around 100 great grandchildren who will likely have at least 200 great-great-grandchildren...and so it goes. PH's siblings and their families were also quite prolific. One might imagine Marquard reunions are a real challenge.

Some of the grandchildren chose to work in the family trades. Vin DeCrane became an architect and head of a well-known contracting and engineering firm. Marquard Electrical Contracting in Rocky River is owned by my Uncle Vin's son James (Deceased 2020) and his wife Kathy Marquard. At least a few of John & Gertie's great grandchildren have a talent for building. The Marquard Remodeling Corporation in Grafton, Ohio is owned by Thomas L. Marquard, the son of Robert and grandson of Lester (1913-1994). Thomas' cousin Shawn owns the Marquard Home Improvement & Remodeling Co. in Fairview Park. He is Jack's son and Lester's grandson.

M.C. (Marquard Company) Real Estate In Medina County, Ohio is a very prominent realty firm, owned by Michael Marquard, wife Nancy and sons Matthew and Brandon. Michael is the son of Richard (Dickie) (1917-1992) and grandson of Fred and Laura's.

It's fair to say that the grandchildren became very successful in their chosen fields. Aunt Verona's son, Al DeCrane Jr., became Chairman and Chief Executive of Texaco Oil Company. Although Al's achievements stand out, they by no means diminish the business success of so many of the grandkids.

The religious side of the family is also well represented. Uncle Vin's daughter, Mary Beth Marquard celebrated her 50th anniversary, in 2013, as a nun in the Order of the Sisters of The Humility of Mary. She is a therapist and spiritual director as well as a consultant for the Cleveland Diocesan Tribunal HM Ministry Center. Elmer Marquard, John's grandson, was ordained a priest in 1966 and retired in 2010. He served various positions of importance including that of Parochial Vicar in Residence at St. John the Evangelist Cathedral in Cleveland.

Another of Vin Marquard's sons, Dennis has been inducted into the National Speedskating Hall of Fame. Fran and Sarah Jane's son David J. Marquard II owns an international healthcare equipment company.

This is a mere sampling of the achievements of the Marquard descendants. With such a large family tree, the branches spread far and wide. I'm sure that their parents, grandparents and great-great-grandparents would be proud of their progeny.

The present generation of Marquards, DeCranes, Faulhabers et al. is a very long list and they, along with future generations, are the true Marquard legacy.

The Big House 2008-2015 (See sad Epilogue)

Great Grandfather Philip's modest pioneer home is in the process of restoration at 4201 Bailey Avenue in Cleveland and PH's and later John's home has been beautifully restored at 2920 Jay Avenue in Cleveland's Ohio City section.

But for me and much of the family, the best reminder of our history still stands (as of this writing) at 3260 Warren Road. One has only to look at the Big House to be reminded of all the stories of our forbears and their achievements.

Being the dreamer that I am, one day I had hoped to buy the house and restore it for use as a restaurant or bed & breakfast. Residing in Michigan, I had friends and relatives in the Cleveland area monitor what had become the Manor House apartments for possible purchase opportunities. Each time an inquiry was made, the owner insisted he wasn't interested in selling. But alas, it slipped through our fingers.

Evidently the property neglect started in the early 1980s

resulting in many tenants moving out. In 2008 the Manor House fell victim to another depression known as the "The Great Recession." Earlier that year one record shows the house and land to be valued at over $333,000, but the old place had fallen into serious disrepair and the owner either couldn't afford or didn't care to make the necessary repairs. Many of the remaining renters vacated the premises. The neglect forced the City of Cleveland to issue code violations and eventually foreclose on the building for back taxes. The City had to vacate the remaining renters but did assist them in finding new housing. The crumbling mansion was put up for sale at a sheriff's auction and eventually sold for a reported $50,000 to St. Mary's Romanian Orthodox Church. The church is its nearest neighbor to the north. Years earlier they had purchased the old Regnatz Dining Hall. They expressed the desire to rehab the home and use it for offices, storage and a Church historical museum. The Spanish-style house next door now serves as the parish house for Pastor Remus Grama and his family. Once all this came to our attention we asked the church officials if they would be interested in reselling. They politely responded that they were not.

The Civil War-era mansion is quite rundown and instead of being the once beautiful landmark, it is now somewhat of an eyesore. Our family that built the house and resided there for so many years would be saddened and ashamed of its appearance. I asked Fr. Grama if he would be amenable to me raising funds and a volunteer workgroup to assist them with the massive undertaking of rehabilitating the building. He was receptive at first to the idea since the church budget was so tight. Fr. Grama also generously granted my request for a tour of the home. He insisted that we limit the number of family-only visitors.

The Manor House Apartments

Inside the Big House

The first trip inside the house took place on a frigid day on January 30, 2010. I was accompanied by my brothers, Phil and Gary, Gary's son Brandon and my late brother Tim's sons, Greg and Drew. None of us had ever been in the old homestead, other than a few visits to the vestibule and foyer area. It was very exciting and somewhat eerie to be able to explore these storied halls and rooms. Father Grama kindly led us through many of the rooms including the basement labyrinth, illuminated only by our flashlights. Drew captured the journey on video and we all took photos. I had brought an album of old pictures so that we might compare the current state of the interior to the images of when our family resided there. The present state was extremely sad compared to its glory days. There was much peeling paint, some water damage and many partitioned walls and doors segregating the apartments that the home had accommodated since 1943. Although the house certainly bears the scars of abuse and neglect, certain areas were somewhat intact such as the living room, music room and especially the "Red Dining Room." A great deal of the Mill's architectural touches remain. The house had been without heat and electricity since 2008 which further added to the deterioration. But on the whole the old place had good bones and seemed pretty sound, considering what it had been through over the last hundred years.

Leaded stain glass
window over staircase.
Mosaic tiled floor in
entryway.
L-R Greg, Phil, Tom,
Drew, Brandon & Gary.
Marquard 1/30/10 tour.

Cap of north pillar.

Paneled wall in former chapel.

Ornate doors off of old ballroom.

Exterior woodwork, note cross.

(2010)

Note the arrows motif of many
of the leaded glass window
designs (2010)

Ghosts?

It was in the "Red Dining Room" near the remains of the built-in china cabinet, where a photo picked up a distinct image of a spectral face on the dark oak paneled wall. Odd white orbs can also be seen in that same photo. To me the face bore a striking resemblance to my father. Others thought it looked like Grandfather. Maybe it was only a weird reflection of one of our own faces. In other rooms some of our photos picked up the same strange white orbs which could not be seen with the naked eye or the lens viewer. During the tour Gary's camera kept turning off and on by itself until the lithium battery was drained. However, after he left the house he checked and the battery was recharged and the camera worked fine.

Adding to the ghost stories, brother Gary had recently presented a framed photo of PH to Cowan's Bar, the former Marquard offices on Lorain Road, which had been requested by the owner, Bill Cowan. The lady tending bar took one look at it and said "That's George!" She went on to explain that she and others had viewed a ghostly figure of an older man sitting at the end of the bar on more than one occasion, usually late at night or after hours. They had named the ghost George and they believe he watches over the building and protects them. The bartender related a story of how one night a patron had too much to drink and became threatening and unruly after being refused further drinks. Before they could call for help, "George" appeared and scared the poor drunk out the door! It is also reported that George is always dressed in an old-time formal suit and they insist that he looks just like Grandfather's portrait!

Gary has also shared other photos of unexplained white orbs as we had seen in the dining room picture, but which he took in the basement of Cowan's Bar. The basement contained a vault where PH locked up money, deeds and other important documents. On another occasion, when Gary was in the basement of the bar, he felt something squeezing his chest and became breathless. As soon as he made it back up the stairs he felt fine again.

Cowan's barmaid says that she has also witnessed a dark smoky spirit that turns the TV off and then on again. This same entity, which she thinks is evil, has smashed drink glasses on the floor at closing time. She added that they have sensed "George" fighting with the evil presence.

The Red Dining Room (2010)

Note the "Ghostface" on the paneling to the right of the old china hutch. Below is an enlargement (2010).

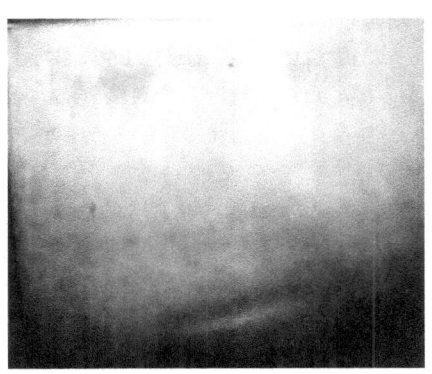

Gary,Tom, Brandon & Greg Marquard 1/30/2010

The Second House Tour

The first tour had to be cut short due to the extreme cold and the fact that an entire wing of the mansion was locked off and Father Grama did not have the needed keys. As a result he granted us another visit on May 4, 2010. On this occasion my cousins Vin DeCrane and Don Faulhaber were able to join us. This was great since they had both spent their childhood under this roof and knew the original layout and history so well. Vin's wife Flo was there as were Uncle Fran's son David and his daughter Victoria and Dave's sister Jane Binzer. Tom Barrett, Dave's sister Joan's husband was also present, as was my nephew Greg. Once again Fr. Grama joined us and Nick Muntean from the church board was there to greet us.

A special guest that day was Uncle Vin's widow Mary

Jane Marquard with son Vincent Jr. Aunt Mary Jane passed away a few years later at age 95. She was the last of my aunts and uncles. It was so nice that she was able to visit the house one last time. On this tour we were able to view the entire home and the grounds. It was great having Vin and Don there as guides and to provide a firsthand account of the origins and usage of each room along with many stories from the era. We located the old chapel and the ballroom and learned many facts about the original floor plan. I have attempted to capture those stories and information within these pages. Prior to the visit Vin DeCrane took the time to draw, from memory, a detailed floor plan of the house and grounds. Considering that he hadn't seen the interior in over 70 years, it was amazing how accurate his sketches were.

Afterward we all gathered in front of the house under the curved portico with the four massive corinthian pillars for a group photograph taken by Fr. Grama. The fact that two of the ornate capitals at the top of those pillars had been replaced by ugly box-like supports attests to the modern day reality of the old mansion.

L-R: Tom B., Fr. Grama, N. Muntean, Don F., Vin M., Tom M., Mary Jane, Flo & Vin D. (5/4/10)

Tom, Greg, Jane, Tom B., Don, Mary Jane, Dave, Victoria, Flo, Vin D., Vin M. and Aunt Mary Jane, also by the old living room fireplace. (5/4/10)

Don Faulhaber and Vin DeCrane comparing notes on the tour.
Below: Vin's diagram of the estate in 1942.

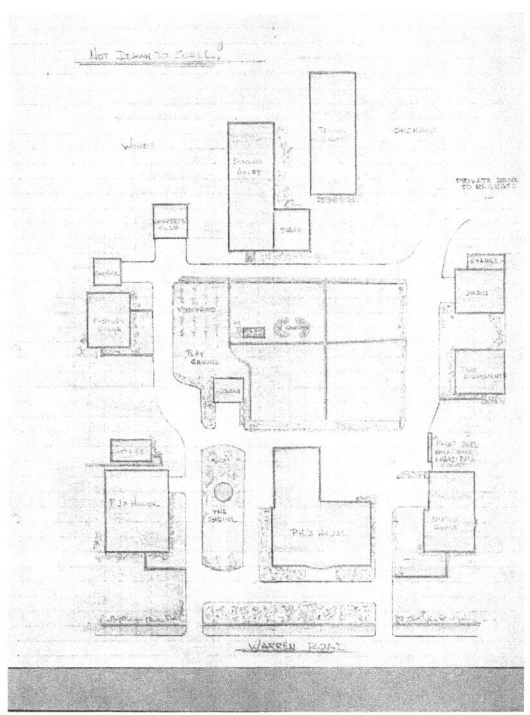

Aunt Mary Jane & Flo in the back of the of house (5/4/10)

Friends of the Big House

Thanks to my brother Gary I was able to connect with the West Park Historical Society back in 2009, The Society had great interest in the house and Gary Swilik had already written a story about it on the WestParkHistory.com website operated by Swilik and Charles Chaney. The Society was concerned over the condition and fate of the landmark and asked me to do a follow-up article on the website's, "History of the West Park Neighborhood." As a result of that website article, I have received dozens of calls and emails from interested West Parkers, former tenants, local history buffs and of course family. Virtually all of them, including the historical society, have volunteered to donate time and/or money to assist in the repair and restoration of the mansion.

I have proffered this assistance to the church many times. Father Grama was interested; however, the church board decided that they did not need outside help and have flatly refused our offers. Unfortunately with budgets being what they are, especially during and after the Great Recession, about all that the church has been able to accomplish, since 2009, was to apply a fresh coat of white paint on the exterior. As of this writing my trepidation grows that the wrecking ball may not be far off.

I applied to the State of Ohio Historical Society to have a historical marker erected in front of the house. After much paperwork and communications, the State enthusiastically approved the marker. Since I was concerned whether St. Mary's would allow the marker on their property, I contacted Cleveland Ward 19 Councilman Martin J. Keane. After several emails and phone conversations I received a letter from Mr. Keane, dated August 24, 2013 expressing his support in having the historical marker placed on the public right–of–way (treelawn) in front of the house. Upon the recommendation of Bob Keiser of the Cleveland Landmark Commission, on June 27, 2013 Mr. Keane introduced a Certificate of Appropriateness to have the city declare the mansion a Cleveland Landmark.

Family, friends and the West Park Historical Society were thrilled that progress had finally been made to recognize the significance of the Big House. Sadly, two years have passed and in spite of my best efforts and those of the historical society and the Kamm's Corners Development Corporation, the City has not completed the steps necessary for the final approval of either the historical marker or the landmark designation. I am unable to finalize the order for the historical marker until the City approves the location site. On April 22, 2015 my application to the National Registry of Historic Places was approved for nomination. I am embarking on that final process next. **(10)**

Final Thoughts

All of my grandparents, parents, uncles and aunts are now gone, but as attested to by these pages, they are far from forgotten. Other than the obvious personal reasons for researching and writing this book, I'm hoping that once readers discover the West Park history enshrouded in the walls of the old manse, renewed interest may be generated to save the home. It is not just the Marquard house but also the Civil War–era farmhouse of the pioneer Brown family. More so, between 1943 and 2008 it was home for hundreds of young Clevelanders, from war workers to today's generation.

After all these years we finally have at least most of the answers to our childhood questions. But it is also my hope that this book will inspire others to come forward with their memories of the family and their "Homes Beautiful".

~ *The End* ~

ACKNOWLEDGEMENTS

Thanks goes to my dad, as well as to my mom, for imparting to us so much of the family lore and for saving the many photos and documents related to that history. Much appreciation goes to Robert J. Marquard (1929–2008) for reaching out to me in 1996 and sharing the family history that his father Wilfred had compiled years before. My dad had a complete copy of that document but it seems to have been lost. Wilfred's history was invaluable in providing a great starting point for my research.

I'm also very grateful to my cousin Vin DeCrane for his immense contributions. In addition to his first–person narrative on the family and the Big House, his excellent sketches of the house and grounds are invaluable. He also gave me Uncle Mark's photo album. His younger sister, and my Godmother, Clarice, was also very helpful in providing her account of life on Warren Road and in identifying the people in many of the old snapshots. It had been many years since I had been in touch with her and it was wonderful to reconnect. Maybe the guiding hand of Grandfather put me up to this work in order to reestablish contact with so many of my relatives whom I had lost touch with since I moved from the Cleveland area in 1972. Vin, Clare and their younger brother Al, were the sole remaining family that remember their time living under that big roof. I was unable to contact Aunt Rita's three daughters but they would have been under the age of five when the house was sold.

Thanks to my other cousins who aided me in this undertaking. Sr. MaryBeth, Ann and Vin Marquard Jr., for sharing their father's old photo album. Ken Marquard did the same with Uncle Dauby's album. Ann Marquard Gilbert also located the photo of Fr. Philip with Martin Luther

King. Dave Marquard aided in sorting out some of the family history. The Faulhaber cousins also provided some great assistance. Especially Alan Faulhaber who was very kind in creating CDs for me of his mother's wedding video and family photo album.

Dave Stack, the current owner of the Jay Avenue home, enthusiastically granted me permission to use his photos of the beautifully restored house. For more photos go to davestack.com/house.

My siblings Phil, Gary, Nancy and sister-in-law Loretta assisted me in this endeavor by sharing their memories. Gary has assumed the position of chief on-the-scene investigator, formerly held by our late brother Tim. Tim's love of family and history continues to inspire us. Tim's sons Greg and Drew follow in his footsteps. They did a great job of recording our tours of the Big House. Nancy's son Ryan is a talented internet researcher, locating archives on Fr. Philip that had eluded us all. I should have enlisted the research help of my nieces and nephews earlier as their generation is much more proficient at it than I. This book should give the family Googlers plenty of fresh leads to track down.

It was so nice to have my Aunt Mary Jane join us for the second tour of the home. She was my sole surviving aunt who, not long after, left us to join her husband and family in the Afterlife. Also along on that second tour was Don Faulhaber, who has since passed away as well. He had many great stories from the good old days. Don gave me his sister Dorie's manuscript 'Tis Better to have Lost, which provided so much rich narrative for this book.

I owe tremendous gratitude to Doris Faulhaber (pictured above). She encouraged me to preserve and record the family history. Her writings, abundantly quoted in this book, have been invaluable. I can't begin to measure up to her writing talent and wit. But, I feel in a way, I have carried on the work she started.

I thank Michael and Shawn Marquard for helping me understand their present day Marquard companies.

I owe a lot to the West Park Historical Society for their help and interest, especially to Ralph Pfingsten, Ross Bassett, Tom McGlynn and Gary Swilik. Gary along with Charles Chaney have a wonderful website WestParkHistory.com full of great information. Gary is also a researcher and author of several terrific West Park history books. As a result of the website dozens of folks have contacted me with stories and to volunteer their support and assistance with any efforts to restore the Big House. I remain very touched by their interest and offers. Maybe one day the church will allow us to help.

It was a rewarding experience working with Laura Herron of the Ohio History Service Corps, Local History Office of the State historical society, in securing the approvals for a State historical marker. I just hope to be able to see it one day at the site of the mansion. I mistakenly thought that the State marker would be the first step in possible recognition by the National Registry of Historic Places. Thanks to the talented freelance journalist Mariam Makatsaria, I learned that the National Registry required a separate application to a different department within the Ohio Historical Society. Mariam put me in touch with Barbara Powers who along with Susan Tietz from the Society kindly aided me in that application. It was deemed to qualify for the Registry on April 22, 2015. Now I have another 14 page final nomination application to complete!

Mariam Makatsaria published a wonderfully insightful and well-researched story on the house in Belt Magazine's June 2, 2015 release, titled: "Preserving Grandeur: Who will save Cleveland's historic Marquard House?" She has my utmost gratitude and respect for the great job she did on the piece. beltmag.com/preserving grandeur/. It has generated quite a bit of interest.

Appreciation goes to Steve Lorenz from the Kamm's Corner Development Commission and Bob Keiser from the Cleveland Landmarks Commission for their assistance and support. I am thankful to City Councilman Marty Keane's support and I'm hoping he'll come through with the approvals needed to erect the historical marker.

Ancestry.com is an amazing resource where I learned so much about my forbears and their families. The site made it possible to connect with my relative and fellow family researcher Sarah Lynne Junke, who provided me with previously unknown and invaluable information on our family's German roots. I had hoped to include the family tree in these pages but it was just too large to accommodate. However I will get the ancestry.com tree updated and share.

The Cleveland Plain Dealer historical archives were a rich source for much of the information contained in this book. I just wish the site was less expensive and a bit more user-friendly.

Our tours of the Big House were made possible by the good graces and approval of the Very Reverend Father Remus Grama, Pastor of St. Mary's Romanian Orthodox Church. He is a wonderful man and a lover of history. I believe he did the best he could have under the circumstances. Nick Muntean, from the St. Mary's Board was also very welcoming to our family at the second tour. I just wish they would accept our many offers of help for the old house and to not swing the wrecking ball.

I owe a world of thanks to my chief editor, proofreader and supporter, my very intelligent, patient and kind wife, Peggy.

Lastly, I wish to apologize for my amateur writing skills and for any factual errors or omissions contained herein, of which I'm sure there are more than a few. Please do not hesitate to bring them to my attention so that I may correct or add to the record. That goes as well for the sources I have probably forgotten to credit and all of those that provided me encouragement to complete this work.

Photos & Images

In the course of sorting and copying hundreds of collected photos from various family sources I lost track of the albums from which many of them originated. Also many of the same pictures were in multiple scrapbooks. Therefore I've credited all family photos as being from "The Marquard Family Collection". Some I noted as such but unless otherwise credited the photos are from the family collection. I sure wish my relatives had identified everyone in the photos along with dates. Most were not, so I estimated and made informed guesses. My apologies for any errors which I likely have made.

Most of the newspaper articles and real estate ads are from the Cleveland Plain Dealer archives. Again some are credited but unless otherwise noted that is the source. Many other news articles were copied from the family scrapbooks.

The cover image of the Big House is a copy of an original watercolor painted by the late, very talented artist, Bruce Dicken (1936–2015). Bruce was Art Director for American Greetings from 1960–1996. In 1964, his associate, Dorie Faulhaber commissioned him to do the painting as well as the one of the Phoenix home which appears in this book. The originals belong to the Faulhaber family. Thank you Mr. Dicken!

Thomas A. Marquard

Dearborn, Michigan
June 2015
tamarquard@icloud.com

(Revisions August 2024)

ABOUT THE AUTHOR

Tom Marquard grew up in Fairview Park, Ohio and after work relocations to Boston in 1972 and Buffalo in 1974 he settled in the Detroit area in 1976. He retired in 2010 after 40 years in the health insurance industry and resides in Dearborn, Michigan with his wife Peggy. He has three wonderful children and five amazing grandchildren.*

Tom's passion for history led him to become the family's historian. Boxes of documents, photos and memorabilia ended up in his possession and he feels it's important to record and share those memories with current and future generations as well as for posterity. His original intent was to put it all down on paper strictly for family. Peggy convinced him to do it in book format and self-publish the valuable memoirs and history.

In 2008 he published his first book with Lulu Press about his great grandfather on his mother's side, "The 1864 Civil War Diary and Brief Biography of James B. Essig." His second book was completed in 2013 based on his Uncle Cyril Marquard's travel journal of the epic 1920 family trip out West, "Trains, Plains & Automobiles," published by CreateSpace, an Amazon company. Since then he has worked exclusively on this book, his most difficult but most rewarding endeavor to date. All three books are available on Amazon.

Tom may be contacted at tamarquard@icloud.com.

* In 2015 Tom and Peggy moved to the Hamburg/Brighton Michigan area.

2025 EPILOGUE

It has been my intention for a number of years to clean up the errors and omissions as well as provide updates to the 2015 edition of this book. Now that I'm finally getting around to it I've realized just how much has changed in the last nine years. Unfortunately much of it is bad news for the story of the "Big House."

In the course of this update I have corrected many minor errors such as typos, without any notation. Major errors or new information generally will have an endnote that can be referenced at the end of this edition.

The "Silent Generation"

We've lost our "Greatest Generation" family members and now the so-called "Silent Generation"—born between 1925 and 1945—are slowly vanishing.

The eldest grandson of Phil & Sophia, Verona and Alfred's first-born, Vincent Francis DeCrane passed away in November of 2022 at the grand old age of 95. Vin led a full life of outstanding service and accomplishments. I've noted throughout the book his many contributions to this story. Vin lost his wonderful and beloved wife of 69 years, Flora (Flo), in March of 2019 at the age of 90. Their enduring legacy consists of 8 children, 27 grandchildren and 20 great grandkids at last count!

We also lost Vin's brother Al DeCrane Jr. at the age of 90 in September of 2021. Al's life achievements and amazing career are legendary and are fully recounted in his obituary. He and his surviving wife of 69 years Joan had 5 children, 16 grandchildren and to date one great-grandchild.

New lost Verona & Al's daughter Clare Walsh in late October of 2024. She had been in an assisted living facility in the Newport Beach, California area. Clare turned

95 on April 18, 2024. Vin's wife, Aunt Mary Jane Marquard holds the current record. She left us in 2012 two days before turning 96. Aunt Honey (Olivia) also made it to within days of her 96th birthday. We all hope to have inherited some of those longevity genes and break the age 95 barrier!

I apologize in advance if I have unknowingly failed to mention other members from our family's "Silent Generation."

"Grandeur of the Past Turned into Rubble"

That was the headline on the front page of the Cleveland Plain Dealer on October 17, 2018. The header by Michelle Jarboe (mjarboe@plaind.com) read "Marquard's mansion unsalvageable." Two days earlier the wrecking crew went to work on the destruction of the beloved old "Big House."

I highly recommend Michelle's article as a great summary of the history and the trials and tribulations suffered by the home and those who loved it.

I do, however, take serious issue with the apparent comments from St. Mary's then parish council president, Vasile Peicu.

Although we made several offers to raise money and provide volunteers to improve the house, the article states "But nobody ever made a formal, written offer to the parish council to buy the property, Peicu said."

That much is true, but only because we were told on more than one occasion that the house was not for sale. As I recall, the last time I pushed on the the possibility of them selling, the sarcastic response I received from Fr. Remus Grama was something to the affect of "Okay how about a million dollars?"

The article went on to say that Peicu stated that they might have sold it for $50,000, which is what they paid for it. If that had been communicated to us this story may have had a dramatically different ending.

For the record, to my knowledge I have never met or communicated with Mr. Peicu nor I'm I aware of any other family member having done so at that time. All of my conversations and meetings were primarily with Fr. Remus Grama and to a lesser extent with Nick Muntean whom I believe was the church board president.

In the final analysis its water under the bridge as the house was razed to the ground. My brother Gary who lives in the area was closely following the news of the impending destruction. With the church's permission he, along with our sister, Nancy Holz and her son Ryan, made one last foray into the house.They managed to salvage quite a bit of the ornamental trim, including doors, leaded glass windows, and mantels both before and after the demolition. Our cousin Vin Marquard Jr. and other relatives and interested parties also retrieved keepsakes and mementoes from the mansion. My daughter Christine Gibson drove down from Michigan but by the time she arrived the site was rubble. Gary and Nancy were kind enough to share some of the salvage with my brother Phil, Christine and myself. One of those beautiful windows is now proudly displayed in our home.

I love the last two paragraphs of Ms. Jarboe's fine article:

"With so many other Marquard-built homes in Cleveland, including much smaller houses flanking the demolition site, the legacy of the now-defunct Marquard Real Estate & Building Co. and the Marquard Sash & Door seem secure.

But Philip H. Marquard's magnum opus is gone."

At our January 10, 2010 tour of the house my late brother Tim's son, Drew, videoed the excursion. The video can be viewed by googling "Marquard Mansion Tour Winter 2010 on Vimeo."

Vanishing Legacy

Unfortunately, other family landmarks have also been bulldozed in recent years.

The old 47,000 square foot <u>Marquard Sash & Door Mfg. Co.</u>at 14735 Lorain Rd. is gone and replaced by a building which now houses Clearvue Insulating Glass Co. I was told that a tool & die company was there previously. I'm not sure when the brick and wood mill was torn down.

The <u>Phil Marquard Real Estate & Building Co. and the Filmar Mortgage Co.</u> office building at 14737 Lorain Rd. erected in 1925 met the wrecking ball in 2021. The building also served as apartments, the Zephyr Bar and most recently as Cowan's Bar. Gary Marquard and other preservationists waged a lively battle to save the landmark but apparently another strip mall and parking lot were more important. The only good news was the developer agreed to save the "Marquard" keystone that adorned the top of the building. **(See page 133)**

""We are paying homage to Marquard by salvaging the keystone and the plaque,"....'Where this building stands, we're incorporating it into the site and working with the CDC to have some public art space.'" (5/7/21 ABC News 5 Cleveland)

Photo by Gary D, Marquard 5/2023

In 1908 Grandfather Marquard purchased the farmhouse at 3260 Warren Road on 7.45 acres of land. By 1914 he expanded his purchase to 14 acres. At his highpoint it is said that he owned up to 50 acres in and around his estate. In 1914 he built a home on the estate for his widowed mother, Mary. She resided there until her death in 1920. Various other family members lived there up until 1943. **(See page 89)**

Grandmother Mary's former home, as well as the nearby family's former old bowling alley building are now slated for removal to make way for 19 townhomes according to an article by Joe Dill in the Spring 2024 edition of "West Park Magazine." However, my brother Gary has told me the project is on hold awaiting an environmental study on the rain runoff plan **as well as purchasing adjacent homes/property to allow for a service** road to the property. Gary along with neighbors are protesting the development by Maverick Building Co.

The Good News

Although we have lost some important family landmarks many more still survive and thrive.

My Great Great Grandparents Philip & Mary's circa 1867 home at 4201 Bailey Ave. in Cleveland is undergoing a slow restoration and remodeling by the current occupants. Brother Gary is keeping tabs on the process and has become acquainted with the owners and toured the home. **(See page 32)**

PH & Sophia's—and later John & Gertrude's—splendid 1902 home at 2920 Jay Ave. in Cleveland remains a masterpiece of restoration thanks to the current owner Dave Stack. **(See pages 41–43)**

Fred & Laura's home at 3276 Warren Rd. Cleveland built in 1911 on the grounds of PH"s estate survives to this day. **(See page 67)**

Great Aunt Julia Marquard & Joseph Battes' beautiful 1896 Marquard-built home at 3221 Carroll Ave. Cleveland is still standing. It has been lived in by their descendants up until the present day! Great grandson Mike Halley is the current owner. My brother Gary met the relatives, toured the home and bought some of the original furnishings. Apparently Mike is rehabbing and remodeling for a possible sale.

Marquard-Battes home (Recent photo)

Newton Avenue homes restoration **(See page 60)** The following is from a 2018 Cleveland Restoration Society newsletter (info@clevelandrestoration.org):

"Drive down Newton Avenue and right away you will understand why this special street is landmarked both locally by the City of Cleveland and listed in the National Register of Historic Places. The block is lined with bungalows which are decorated with architectural features pulling from Colonial and Classical Revival designs that are often found on larger, high-style homes. The effect is charming, the homes are well-kept, and the cohesive design of the block makes one appreciate this gem of a street. Jerry Maddox was the person behind the effort to nominate Newton Avenue to the National Register of

Historic Places in 1988, and likely the local designation as a Cleveland Historic District that same year.

Jerry acquired Newton Avenue houses because he deeply appreciated their architectural significance, and he wanted to ensure their survival. He was very worried that Newton Avenue would be consumed by institutional expansion. The houses on Newton Avenue were constructed between 1910 and 1923, developed by the Marquard companies who became well-known for their designs of small homes with details found in larger and more expensive homes. These Marquard homes have many wonderful interior features such as solid wood doors with varying designs and decorative trims; wood windows with divided lights in different patterns such as diamonds and ovals; and leaded glass windows, some clear and some with color. Interior features include elaborate wood trim, ceiling beams, paneling, built-in cupboards with leaded glass window and doors, and fireplace alcoves with built-in benches."

The good news is that the restorations were a huge success and the homes are lived in once again!

9800 Newton Avenue   9801 Newton Avenue   9805 Newton Avenue   9804 Newton Avenue

First Families Certificate

In the summer of 2018 The West Park Historical Society awarded "First Families" framed certificates to members who have proven direct descendancy to ancestors who resided in the city of West Park prior to January 1923 when it was annexed to Cleveland. Brother Gary and I were among the first to receive the certificates thanks to our grandparents Philip Henry and Sophia Helen (Lindenau) Marquard who took up residency as early as 1908.

Marquard Brothers Receive First Families of West Park Certificates

Our prestigious First Families of West Park certificates were awarded to brothers Gary and Thomas Marquard at the end of August.

The brothers met all requirements of being society members in good standing and directly descended from an ancestor who resided within the independent City of West Park before January 1, 1923 – when West Park was annexed and became part of Cleveland. Gary and Thomas are direct descendants of Phillip Henry Marquard, a prolific builder of West Park homes and buildings.

For an application or inquiries regarding First Family of West Park recognition, email us at WestParkHS@gmail.com.

West Park resident and WPHS Board Member Gary Marquard receiving his First Family of West Park certificate from WPHS President Steve Lorenz.

West Park
HISTORICAL SOCIETY

Gary D. Marquard

FIRST FAMILIES OF WEST PARK

Philip Henry Marquard

New Books

My brother Gary has really taken up the family historian mantle since his retirement. He has spent countless hours researching our family tree as well as visiting and photographing Marquard-built homes and landmarks. More importantly he has located and contacted dozens of our second and third cousins scattered across the Cleveland metro area. In doing so he has established new relationships and unearthed new family history. As a result, he planned and organized two separate "Cousins" reunions!

His research has culminated in his authoring and publishing two books. Both are available on Amazon.

The Phil Marquard Real Estate & Building Company: A Historic Book of Then And Now (2021). The book is loaded with hundreds of historic images as well as current photos of Marquard-built homes.

Generations (2023) This book tells our family story using hundreds more images, news articles and photos.

Gary is also longtime member and former trustee of the West Park Historical Society. As such he has volunteered many hours to that fine organization.

In 2023, I edited and published a book based on manuscripts written by my late cousin Doris j. Faulhaber. It also is available on Amazon.

'Tis Better To Have Lost is Dorie's biographical coming-of-age story and her lifelong battle with obesity and self-doubt. The story is told with her special brand of wit and humor.

Dorie was born in 1929 and spent a mostly idyllic

childhood living in the Marquard "Big House." Her story narrates life during the Great Depression and World War II, including the loss of beloved relatives as well as the family fortune. The post–war years cover her school day adventures, humorous jobs and occupational hazards.

Woven throughout her story are the often sad but usually entertaining tales of the good, the bad and the ugly of obesity, diets and doctors.

As an addendum, I included in the book her loving and tragic story of our uncle...

A Short Biography of Lt. David J. Marquard (1948)

Many thanks to all those who helped to correct the record, including Sara Junke, Sr. Mary Beth Marquard, Ann Gilbert, Vin DeCrane, Gary Marquard, Leo Marquard and others.

Additional comments, corrections etc. may be sent to me at tamarquard@icloud.com.

Thomas Austin Marquard
Hamburg Township, Michigan
January 2025

ENDNOTES

1. **Page 19**. All of our American records show my fraternal 3x great grandfather John's middle name to be **Frederick** or don't show a middle name or initial. Sara Junke's research into the German records indicate it was actually **"Nepomuk."** This was a fairly common name at the time in that part of Europe. Johannes Nepomuk (1345–1393) was a Saint and martyr of Bohemia. I'm guessing that since that name is quite foreign in America John may have changed it to "Frederick" which could have been a Confirmation name. I located some family trees that show Great Grandma Mary's father's name as Jan (John) Nepomuk Cerny!

2. **Page 20**. John's father was Josephus Marquard (1772–1846) He married in 1794 to Maria Lucia Vogtle (abt 1768–1806). Joseph & Lucia were my 4X great grandparents. After Maria's death he remarried in 1806 to Maria Anna Hochsbach, (John's stepmother). Records indicate that Josephus' father was Sebastianus (B. Abt 1747) and mother was Theresia Kefl (sp.) which would make them my 5x fraternal great grandparents. According to Ms. Junke, it looks like they were married in 1768 and had a "bunch" of children starting in 1769. German baptismal records indicate that Sebastianus' father's name was also Sebastianus and his mother's name was Regina Mogg. Maria Lucia Vogtle's father was Andreas and mother was Catharina Neusch. For further details and clarity I intend to update my family tree on Ancestry.com. John's wife Anna's father was Philip Loffler. It's entirely probable that their son Philip was named for him and thus started the Marquard line of "Philips." Of course, PH was named for his father and so on down the line. So this would make Philip David the 5th Philip Marquard in our line.

3. **Page 24**. Sarah Junke located and shared with me John's last Will & Testament dated March 26,1862 as well as the Probate Court records dated March 27, 1862. No middle name or initial is shown. The records show that John left the house and all of the furnishings to Ursula and that she was to have been responsible for the upkeep, taxes etc. The house and furnishings would go to the children upon Ursula's death or remarriage. According to the 1888 City

Directory, Ursula Marquard was still there and listed as the widow of John. However, records show she remarried in 1867 to Charles Frei, a neighborhood saloonkeeper. Evidently the 1888 directory is incorrect as the 1872 directory shows her working at the saloon. The 1894 probate & will records show her surname as Frei with no husband and leaving everything to her only daughter Mary Haug Grotzinger. Upon her remarriage, the house and furnishings should have passed immediately to John's children including step-daughter, Mary Haug Grotzinger. Yet city directory records from 1880,1891 and 1895 show her as Ursula Frei <u>not</u> Marquard and as the widow of Charles Frei and still residing at 30 Ash. In conclusion, it appears she somehow found a way to stay in the house. We don't know how she managed to retain ownership and therefore left it to her daughter. Possibly she bought it from from the children? It certainly sounds like a recipe for dissension among her and/or the children.

4. **Pg 39.** Due to controversy, Cleveland's baseball team dropped the Chief Wahoo logo in 2018. In 2021 the team team officially changed their name from the Indians to the Guardians. Also headdresses and warpaint were banned in the stadium.

5. **Pg 102.** The sale of the Phoenix home/Verona Apartments in 1927 for $75,000 would equate to about $1.3 million in 2024 dollars.

6. **Pg 126** Upon further review, I can't say with certainty that the photo was taken in the Big House rathskeller. Based on the absence of Cleo, Phil and David, I'm dating it at the earliest to mid-1942 to mid-1944, as they would have been off in the service. Also the presence of Ginny Weidt, David's fiancé, would put it prior to his death. If it was the rathskeller it would have had to be prior to 11/15/42 when the estate sale took place and before 6/22/44 when David was killed in action. Maybe it was a final farewell_party to the rathskeller and the Big House? Another theory is the photo may have been from Schluters catering hall in Westlake, Ohio where the Marquards had many family reunions—usually around the Christmas season—in many of the years after the Big House was sold.

7. **Pg 229.** In Sept 2018 Peggy and I toured Normandy and thanks to the Utah Beach historian, Benoit Noel, we were able to follow both Dave and Cleo's footsteps from those fatal days. Dave's outfit was the first to land in Normandy and Cleo's hospital unit followed on D–Day +4. We were able to visit the actual sites from the beach to the location where Uncle Dave lost his life and the site of the former American Cemetery where he was interred for three years. We saw where Uncle Cleo's hospital group was located and even visited the church where Cleo prayed. Below is a photo of the church where Cleo prayed and the site of the 91st Hospital Evacuation Group.

8. **(Pg 258)** I previously thought that the Mill burned down but the fire was evidently at the Forest City Materials building next door. Although the Sash & Door was damaged, the building and land were purchased and/or leased for a number of years until it was torn down and replaced by a modern structure.

9. **(Pg 259)** As I recall, **Esther Smith** was the secretary at the Marquard Building Co. after it relocated to Fairview Park. She also was a wonderful person who put up with all of our phone calls and visits to Dad. In my mind she seems interchangeable with Mary Ann Brennan. Both lovely and efficient ladies.

10. **(Pg 280)** Although approved by the state, the historical marker never came to fruition. Even though we planned to finance it—including its maintenance—after much delay and many excuses it was not to be. I think the church's objection and local politics prevented it from happening in spite of the tree lawn being considered public property. With the house now gone the marker's wording was such that it would still be appropriate to the site.

PERSON INDEX
(Edited 2025)

Note: Philip Henry Marquard is omitted as he appears in most of the content. Also names on images are not included herein.

Marquard continued...

NOTES